Venturing abroad
in Asia

Venturing abroad in Asia

The complete business guide
to cultural differences
in eleven Asian countries

Robert T. Moran

McGRAW-HILL BOOK COMPANY

London · New York · St Louis · San Francisco · Auckland
Bogotá · Guatemala · Hamburg · Lisbon · Madrid · Mexico New
Delhi · Panama · Paris · San Juan · São Paulo · Singapore
Sydney · Tokyo · Toronto

Published by
McGRAW-HILL Book Company (UK) Limited
MAIDENHEAD · BERKSHIRE · ENGLAND

British Library Cataloguing in Publication Data

Moran, Robert T.
    Venturing abroad in Asia: the complete business guide to the
    cultural differences in eleven Asian countries.
    1. Asia. — Visitors' guides
    I. Title
    915'.04428

ISBN 0-07-707098-4

Cover illustration by Jonathan Planner

Printed in Great Britain by
Butler & Tanner Ltd., Frome and London.

INTRODUCTION

In my 25 years of travel in the global business community, nothing has ever quite matched the poignance of a scene I once witnessed in Tokyo. A Japanese executive was singing "Melancholy Baby" to his European business partner in a hostess bar on the Ginza. The singer-businessman put his best efforts into the song, copying the crooners' moves by placing hand on heart, and even managing a little break in the voice. "Melancholy Baby" was an alien sound to him — and to the guest — but as a culture-bridging gesture it was heroic. Although in the end, it was hard to tell who was more embarrassed, the singer or his guest.

What was going on here? An English lesson? Gross exhibitionism? No, it was merely a Japanese "ice-breaking" tradition in which the host and guests each make a public performance of some sort, usually in song, to create a bond among the members of a group. The choice of a sentimental tune from the 1940s was less than artful, but the intention was pure as the driven snow. The Japanese executive was attempting to meet his guest more than halfway.

In business relations that mix unfamiliar cultural traditions, anything that eases the strain is worth trying. The singing executive in Tokyo was going out of his way to be hospitable, for normally the burden of bridging the cultural gap rests on the visitor, not the host.

Nowhere is this gap wider and more treacherous than between East and West, between the Asian cultures and those of Europe and the Americas. And nowhere in the widening sphere of international business is the increased pace of interaction as rapid. Japan and the "new Japans" of South Korea, Taiwan, Singapore, Hong Kong, Thailand, and, to a lesser extent, Malaysia and Indonesia, have become ever-present economic forces in the daily lives of every Westerner. Tomorrow, China and India, with their gigantic populations, will make themselves felt. No longer is it possible to avoid exposure to the business influence emanating from Asia.

Fortunately or unfortunately, depending upon your aptitude for absorbing the fine points of each country's ways, global business and the exportation of American television entertainment have not disturbed the individuality that makes each Asian country a delight in its own way. In this book, Prof. Robert T. Moran analyzes each of 11 Asian cultures from the perspective of the business visitor. As a handbook for first-time travellers to Asia, or as a reference work for frequent visitors, the book serves as an explanatory guide for Westerners.

Dr. Moran has devoted his professional life to the study of cultural differences among peoples. His expertise is sought by business executives in seminars and conferences throughout the world. And readers of *International Management* have followed his regular column since 1985.

Venturing Abroad is the first handbook of its kind — a cultural compendium for the Western business traveller in Asia. It has the potential to ease the visitor's entry into each country. Dr. Moran takes you behind the mysteries of the East.

Michael Johnson
Editor-in-Chief
International Management
London

September, 1988

Dedication

I dedicate this book to six people I love and admire very much. All are now learning another language and way of life in a country far from where they were born.

I dedicate this book to Virgilia, my spouse, partner and friend; to Elizabeth, Sarah, Molly and Rebecca, my daughters; and to Benedict, my son.

Acknowledgements

"There are truths on this side of the Pyrenees that are falsehoods on the other." So said the great philosopher Pascal many years ago.

The purpose of this book is to identify the important business truths, customs and courtesies in 11 different countries in Asia. It is my belief that the manager of today, and even more so in the future, must know how other business systems work and possess the skills to work effectively in these environments. This is so because of the rapid proliferation of different forms of business alliances between organizations and enterprises in different countries.

Many people contributed to the research required to write this book. I wish to particularly acknowledge and thank Michael Buenning, Scott Donnellan, Cheryl Kern, Lania Larenz, Gregory Nobles, Geralyn Porch and Regina Whitley, all graduate assistants at American Graduate School of International Management.

I also wish to thank Barbara Starr, who has been my secretary for the past nine years. She not only typed and retyped the entire manuscript, she also carefully read the material and made many good suggestions to improve its readability.

CONTENTS

Venturing abroad in Asia

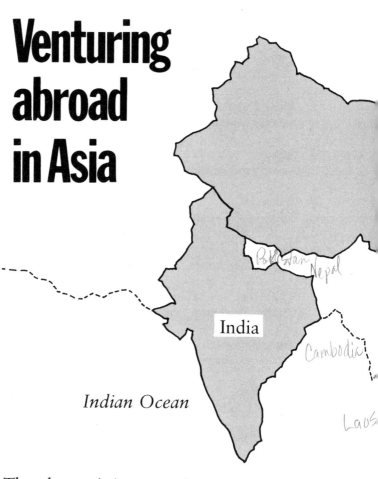

The eleven Asia countries
covered in this business guide

Kilometres
0   1000   2000

CHINA

Tomorrow's powerhouse

Probably the most difficult of all business cultures for a Westerner to master is that of China. The blend of warm hospitality and cold, calculating business practice can be seen at first to be contradictory. Actually, the Chinese are simply uncompromising on the essentials of any deal: they will always choose the option they think is best for China. What is best for China is not always clear and there are many competing interests of city vs. province vs. state.

The Chinese expect foreign businessmen to be highly qualified in their areas of expertise. Chinese businessmen do not feel the need to show their intellectual expertise or to make an impression on the foreign guest. Yet the foreign businessman who is worthy and a true professional will have discreet but lavish attention showered on him while he is in China.

In social life as in business, the Chinese traditionally place great emphasis on proper etiquette. Foreign businessmen should demonstrate, in return, dignity, reserve, patience, persistence and a sensitivity to Chinese customs and temperament. Efficiency and punctuality, and the value of work are paramount. All things being equal, the Chinese generally give preference to companies having long-standing relationships with state trading companies, however, the deal on offer is the key factor. Newcomers have to adjust to the slower, more deliberate Chinese style of making contacts, negotiating and arranging for contracts.

The Chinese seem very relaxed at mixing their duties with gossip, talk about basic amenities, and a steady intake of tea. But they generally work six days a week, with only six national holidays a year.

1

The Chinese rank among the toughest negotiators in the world. A typical invitation to visit China on business might be as follows: "We are glad to inform you that two of your proposed topics have been accepted. Please send 25 copies of your papers one month prior to your arrival. Please send immediately the names of your company's representatives, their biographies, their nationalities and their passport numbers."

Technical competence is a primary criterion for the representatives. A number of Western companies have been obliged to leave China midway through a visit and return later with more technically seasoned engineers.

The size of the negotiating team sent to China is generally from two to seven people, but varies depending on the circumstances. One person should be appointed leader and should serve as the official spokesman for the visiting team. The Chinese prefer to deal with senior people who are able to make decisions during the trip.

It is essential that the foreign businessman be patient because negotiations often run for ten days straight and can become very tedious and tiresome. The chief negotiator of the Boeing team that sold $125 million worth of 707s to China in the 1970s spent a total of 100 days in Beijing. The Chinese very often ask detailed questions that do not seem to be important. In preparing for a presentation, the foreign negotiator should be well-versed in all aspects of his products or services.

Invariably, the Chinese negotiators are extremely well prepared. Although business negotiations usually start slowly and stiffly, both sides gradually relax, and discussions become more informal.

Visitors will probably be invited to a restaurant by the organization sponsoring the visit. The guest should arrive on time or a bit early. The host normally toasts the guest at an early stage in the meal, with the guest reciprocating after a short interval. Alcoholic beverages should not be drunk until a toast has been made. It is the custom to toast each course. At the end of the dinner, the guest of honour makes the first move to depart. The usual procedure is to leave shortly after the meal is finished. Most business dinners end by 9 o'clock in the evening.

It is important to return invitations if they are given. If a banquet is given in honour of the visiting group, the visitors should organize a banquet for the Chinese team. Small company souvenirs or books often make acceptable presents; expensive gifts do not.

Mandarin (or Putonghua) is the official language of China, but Cantonese is spoken in the south by more than 150 million people. The study of English as a second language has been widely encouraged. Businessmen will find that the people with whom they negotiate either speak English or have interpreters available. The Chinese Travel Service can advise businessmen on reliable translation services.

Foreign companies are advised not to bring their own interpreter unless this person is also technically competent. The quality of the Chinese interpreters varies. If the translation seems unsatisfactory, a word to the leader of the Chinese delegation will be enough to secure a replacement interpreter.

On January 1, 1979, China adopted officially the "pinyin" system of writing Chinese characters in the Latin alphabet. This is a system of romanization invented by the Chinese that has been widely used for years in China on street signs, as well as in elementary Chinese textbooks. Pinyin is now to replace the familiar Wade-Giles romanization system. The following are examples of the Wade-Giles and pinyin systems:

Wade-Giles	Pinyin
Peking	Beijing
Canton	Guangzhou
Mao Tse-tung	Mao Zedong
Teng Hsiao-ping	Deng Xiaoping
Hua Kuo-feng	Hua Guo Feng
Chou En-lai	Zhou En Lai

Historical Context

China has one of the world's oldest continuous civilizations. The origins of the state can be traced back as far as 2000 B.C. Early China was characterized by warring feudal states that were not unified until the Qin Dynasty (221-206 B.C.). Numerous dynasties, both Chinese and non-Chinese, developed the imperial system in China. In 1911, the Manchu or Qing Dynasty was overthrown by the popular revolution of Sun Yat-sen.

During the 1920s, Chiang Kai-shek tried to reunite, under his Nationalist government, a country increasingly fragmented and regionally controlled. Sporadic civil war between Nationalist forces and Communist forces took place from the 1920s until 1949, when the Communist forces, led by Mao Zedong succeeded in forcing the National Party of Chiang Kai-shek onto the island of Taiwan.

In the 1950s, close ties were forged with the Soviet Union and economic modernization began in earnest. In 1956, all commercial and manufacturing companies were converted to state-owned and state-controlled operations.

In 1960, dissension developed between Mao and Soviet leader Nikita Khrushchev. The Soviets pulled out entirely from the China industrial aid programme, leaving China's industrialization plans severely impeded.

For a time, a less radical group of leaders retrenched somewhat from Mao's more radical ideas. But in 1966 Mao made a comeback, leading the Great Proletarian Cultural Revolution, purging the government of tens of thousands of officials.

Opening to the West

In the early 1970s, China retreated from the radical extremes of the Cultural Revolution. Overtures were made to the United States, and President Nixon made his historic visit to China in 1972. Efforts have been made to open China further to trade relations with the non-communist world.

Today China totals about 1 billion people, a quarter of the world's population.

The name "China" translates as "middle Kingdom", for the Chinese viewed themselves, their country and their culture as the centre of human civilization. In the past, the Chinese expected that all other peoples and nations would pay tribute and homage to them.

In 1949, following the establishment of The People's Republic of China, the Chinese Communist Party attempted to effect basic changes in attitudes, values and behaviour of the

Chinese. The purpose of Mao Zedong and his reformers was to give the country new direction and build from a traditional feudalistic society to a modern, socialistic one.

A fundamental tool in effecting these changes in basic Chinese values was the development of a people's democracy in which each and every individual — from peasant farmer to high government official — would regularly take a part in the decision-making process at all levels. To accomplish this, work crews, communities, factory organizations and schools were organized into study teams as a part of the daily business to investigate the socialistic principles upon which the government was established. In attempting to make these changes, four major areas were identified as obstacles to overcome:

1) The reduction of the difference in economic and political development of urban and rural areas.
2) The reduction of economic and political inequality between the industrial and peasant workers.
3) The reduction of inequality between manual labourers and the élite.
4) The reduction of inequality between the sexes.

The Chinese people became even more involved in the politics of their nation during two major historical events. These were The Great Leap Forward in the late 1950s and The Cultural Revolution of the late 1960s. During these two periods, economic efficiency and social order were forsaken as the country embarked on major new programmes designed to eliminate "revisionist" elements and to illustrate to the people the importance of their role.

Since normalization of relationships with the West, a great deal of water has flowed along the Yangtze River and the number of foreign business people and others visiting China has steadily increased.

China is attempting to respond to problems of low productivity, obsolete technology, and other issues affecting their drive to increase the average monthly wage from US$40 to over US$1,000 per year by the year 2000.

The birth rate has remained a major problem. The government hopes to stabilize the population at 1.3 billion people by the year 2040. During Mao's years, population growth was encouraged, as Mao proclaimed that people were the nation's richest resource, and that all would share in growing and bountiful wealth. Now the government is legally enforcing birth control.

China is governed under the new constitution formally adopted in 1982. Under the provisions of the constitution, the highest order of state power is the National People's Congress (NPC). Deputies are elected from every region in China for five-year terms. The NPC then elects the head of state, the president of the PRC. They also elect the State Council, which administers the country. The State Council comprises the premier, two vice-premiers, ministers and heads of various state agencies.

The Chinese Communist Party controls all government functions. Membership exceeds 40 millon. The infrastructure at the local and regional levels parallels that of the government structure. The highest authority of the party resides in the National Party Congress. The NPC elects a Central Committee which in turn elects a Politburo. Those who belong to the Politburo are the country's top leaders.

The Chinese people are non-religious but are influenced by Taoism, Confucianism and Buddhism. The constitution of their government states atheism to be the official "religion".

The economy
The nation's economy still depends chiefly upon agriculture, and farming remains the leading industry. Agricultural products account for more than half the value of all the goods produced in China.

China imports wheat from Australia and Canada; machinery and steel from Japan; and chemicals, plastics and textiles from France. Such products as textiles, raw silk and soybeans make up about half of China's exports.

It is the world's largest producer of rice and tobacco and also of vegetable crops. It ranks second in the production of corn and cotton and is the third largest producer of tea and wheat. China is also the world's largest hog and sheep producing nation. Its fishing industry is among the largest in the world, with about 5.4 million metric tons of fish and shellfish caught per year.

The country has great mineral wealth, the most important

minerals being coal, iron ore and the ores of antimony, manganese, tin and tungsten.

Trade has been decentralized to some extent, and individual states now compete fiercely for foreign business and investment. Many foreign businesses have complained of confusion over whom to deal with. Among obstacles to trade are the bureaucracy, low productivity of workers, lack of education, and lack of clear laws regarding foreign trade. The best prospects for trade with or investment in China are compensation trade, joint ventures, barter and buy-back trade or straight purchases from China.

In the coming years, implementation of the seventh Five-Year Plan will dominate the economy. Having abandoned the constraints of the Maoist commune system in the rural economy, the Chinese leadership now faces the more difficult task of instituting similar changes in the urban sectors, despite opposition.

Widespread implementation of the reforms will reduce central government control and decrease the Soviet-style highly centralized economy. A more liberal market-oriented system should replace it, eventually leading to a new political and social structure.

China's economy was planned to expand by 6-8% a year from 1986 to 1990, compared with the 8.4% average annual growth rate from 1981 to 1985.

Tight credit and foreign exchange controls prompted by high inflation and the large trade deficit of 1985 restrained investment and import expansion in the short run.

Growth in the agricultural sector will decelerate during the years 1986-90 to about 5% compared with more than 11% recorded over 1981-85. Agriculture's share of GDP will fall from 36.7% in 1985 to about 34% by 1990.

The government foresees a partial switchover to a free-market economy. Although the government will retain control over macroeconomic factors, microeconomic matters will be determined by market forces. Factories will pay the government a fee roughly equivalent to a corporate tax and retain the rest of the profits for reinvestment and worker incentives and bonuses. Prices will also be gradually decontrolled in line with World Bank recommendations.

Labour problems are major and growing. The government announced that it can no longer provide jobs for all of those seeking employment, and it will guarantee jobs only for technical school or college graduates. This is going to encourage private sector self-employed labour, prohibited during the Cultural Revolution. Of the 40 million who enter the labour force each year, an estimated 2 million will now be self-employed. Corruption is widespread, and is considered by some businessmen to be the single most difficult problem for the Westerner to handle. But despite excesses in the factory-run bonus system, productivity has increased somewhat, and the competition for jobs is also likely to stimulate worker productivity, which is estimated to be about half that of Hong Kong workers. The government has also enacted laws to allow foreign firms to hire, fire and promote, with their decisions based on individual performance. But there is still a long way to go before China makes full use of its manpower.

Infrastructure is seriously underdeveloped. Roads are poor, and there are frequent electricity shortages. Telecommunications systems are primitive, and much of the housing is poor. This has deterred some foreign investment.

Bibliography

Barnett, A. Doak, *China and the Major Powers in East Asia*. Washington, D.C.: Brookings, 1977.

Boarman, Patrick M. and Jayson Mugar, *Trade with China*. Los Angeles: Center for International Business, 1973.

Bonavia, D., *The Chinese*. New York: Lippincott, 1980.

Brandt, Conrad, Benjamin Schwartz, and John K. Fairbank, *A Documentary History of Chinese Communism*. New York: Atheneum, 1971.

Fairbank, J.K., *The United States and China* (Fourth Edition). Cambridge, MA: Harvard University Press, 1979.

Fairbank, John K., *China Perceived: Images and Policies in Chinese-American Relations*. New York: Knopf, 1974.

Fraser, J., *The Chinese: Portrait of a People*. New York: Summit Books, 1980.

Frolic, M.B., *Mao's People*. Cambridge, MA: Harvard University Press, 1980.

Harding, Harry, Jr., *China and the U.S.: Normalization and Beyond*. The China Council of the Asia Society and the Foreign Policy Association, 1979.

Hinton, H.C., editor, *The People's Republic of China: A Handbook*. Boulder, CO: Westview, 1980.

Hsiao, Gene T., *The Foreign Trade of China: Policy, Law and Practice*. Berkeley: University of California Press, 1977.

Hsu, Francis L.K., *Americans and Chinese*. Garden City, N.Y.: Doubleday, Natural History Press, 1972.

Kaplan, Frederick, et al., *Encyclopedia of China Today*. Fair Lawn, N.J.: Eurasian Press, 1979.

Lo, R.E. and K.S. Kinderman, *In the Eye of the Typhoon*. New York: Harcourt Brace Jovanovich, Inc., 1980.

Oxnam, Robert B. and Richard C. Bush, editors, *China Briefing 1981*. Boulder, CO: Westview Press, 1981.

Pye, Lucian W., *Asian Power and Politics*. Cambridge, MA: Harvard University Press, 1985.

Pye, Lucian W., *Chinese Commercial Negotiating Style*. Cambridge, MA: Oelgeschlager, Gunn & Hain Publishers, 1982.

Szuprowicz, Bohdan and Maria, *Doing Business with the People's Republic of China: Industries and Markets*. New York: John Wiley & Sons, 1978.

Townsend, J.R. and R.C. Bush, editors, *The People's Republic of China: A Basic Handbook*. New York: The China Council of the Asia Society and the Council.

HONG KONG

Double Haven Bay in New Territories

Land of nuance

Hong Kong...the name (meaning <u>Fragrant Harbour</u>) brings to mind many varied images: a teeming throng of people, most of whom are Chinese; one of the most beautiful natural harbours in the world, with vistas that leave one breathless; and a vital commercial/industrial centre that is immensely overcrowded and at the same time fascinating and intriguing. Enigmatic, energetic, eastern, British and always exciting, the Crown Colony of Hong Kong is probably the most interesting business location in Asia.

Perhaps the most useful tip for working with Hong Kong Chinese is to bear in mind the concept of <u>"face"</u>. <u>Because disagreement and disharmony are frowned upon in Eastern cultures, a Chinese will reply to questions or requests with the answer he believes is expected.</u> You must listen for the nuances to understand what is actually meant. When the Chinese businessman might be trying to say no, hesitation or caution are the signals to be aware of. The Chinese people place a higher <u>emphasis on courtesy than on accuracy</u> in their everyday transactions. <u>To criticize, point out an error or otherwise challenge a Chinese during business negotiations will be considered discourteous and cause him to lose face.</u>

Although the Chinese do not relish criticism, they are not reluctant to express it themselves. Should a third party be criticized during a discussion, the best course is to talk positively about the situation in general. <u>Agreeing with criticism of a Chinese can place you in disfavour.</u>

Despite the low status accorded merchants in the traditional Chinese hierarchy, in Hong Kong businessmen are highly regarded. The Hong Kong Chinese see hard work and fruitful business dealings as a way of improving one's life. They are certainly excellent businessmen and tough bargainers.

Until recently, "tea money" has been helpful in getting business negotiations to go your way. Everyone, from repair men and delivery people upwards, responds favourably to a little extra "tea money". Over the past few years, however, such payments to get a job done correctly and quickly have been on the decline, owing in part to the establishment in 1973 of the Independent Commission Against Corruption (ICAC). Many people from both the public and private sectors have been successfully prosecuted by the ICAC, and there is a Prevention of Bribery Ordinance that has a clause specifically designed for the private sector prohibiting acceptance of any commissions, rebates or other "advantages" without special permission from the employer or principal of the firm concerned.

From the hustle and bustle of central Hong Kong it is not apparent, but the Chinese businessman often takes more time to make decisions than his Western counterpart. He does not appreciate being pushed or forced to make a decision and considers the use of such tactics shifty. Complimentary courtesy calls and personal selling are effective ways of increasing the chances for business success. All important business should be done face-to-face if possible.

Make it perfectly clear
Though there should be little difficulty in communicating with most businessmen, the problem of exactly how to express a thought or idea is a recurrent one. Idiomatic expressions such as "six of one, half a dozen of the other" should be avoided. When dealing with traditional manufacturers it may be necessary to resort to an interpreter, but speaking slowly and clearly is usually sufficient.

Never talk about failure, poverty or death, especially around the Chinese New Year. The Chinese are very superstitious and even the mention of the possibility of failure or misfortune offends their sensibility.

Superstition also plays a large part in the construction and operation of business facilities. The concept of *feng shui*

(Cantonese for air-water) means that there are natural elements that control or affect the luck of a particular location. Sometimes when considering the purchase or construction of a new building, the Chinese may consult *feng shui* men before making the final decision.

Words which should be avoided are those which imply Western superiority or colonial influence, such as "underdeveloped nation", "Westernize", "Far East" or "native".

"Far" East gives a colonial impression because in the past it was used to mean "far from London". "Southeast Asia" refers to Thailand, Burma, Malaysia, Singapore, the Philippines and Indonesia; "East Asia", Japan, Korea, China, Taiwan and Hong Kong. The "Sub-continent" refers to India, Pakistan, Bangladesh and Sri Lanka. Any of the above terms are acceptable as long as they are used *correctly*.

"Asiatic" is another word with colonial significance that should not be used. The preferred term is "Asian". A most hated and derogatory term is "*native*" since it, too, was used in colonial days. The Asian people as a whole feel it is patronizing.

When referring to Hong Kong or any Asian country, appropriate terminology is "modernizing", "newly developed" and words with technological associations that connote progress.

Examples of English translations of Cantonese words that could lead to some embarrassment are:

1. "Chicken" (easily confused with the American "chick") means prostitute.
2. "Turtle" also has obscene connotations when translated into Chinese.
3. Yellow is the Chinese equivalent of blue in "blue movies", but the colour yellow can be worn with no problem.

The pace of life in Hong Kong is only slightly less frantic than in New York or London. However, Hong Kong Chinese follow the traditional Asian ways of doing things at their own pace and discretion. Business is a very important part of life and it is taken seriously. Meetings and appointments generally take place on time, although subordinate staff can wait as long as 30 minutes for senior staff should the latter be late. The Chinese businessman's punctiliousness also extends to the areas of contracts and contract fulfilment. Until recently, he considered

12

his word as his bond and the honouring of an oral contract as a matter of personal integrity. Now contracts with Western businessmen are written.

The traditional Chinese greetings are usually more reserved than the Western shaking of hands, though the gesture is quite widely accepted. Embraces should be avoided. Should a large number of people be involved in the greeting, it is customary to begin with the eldest person first and end with the youngest. Acceptable topics for conversation are health (especially complimenting the fine health of an elderly person) and school. Asking questions about the family in first business meetings should probably be avoided, although after the first meeting a polite inquiry is acceptable. In business conversation, the Chinese are not at all reluctant to talk about money and/or profits.

An invitation to dinner from a friend or business associate should not be taken lightly. Chinese business dinners are usually all-male affairs. Formal dinners will consist of approximately 12 courses, beginning with a cold dish followed by a soup and ending with fried rice or noodles (and possibly a fruit dish). All dishes should be finished except the last, for to do that would make the host think you are still hungry. Learning to eat with chopsticks is essential. After the meal the chopsticks should be placed neatly on the table, not across the mouth of any dish.

Imbibing in moderation

Alcohol consumption is significant, but heavy drinking is frowned upon, especially at business luncheons. When invited to the home of a Chinese, it is customary to bring a small gift (brandy is especially appreciated). The same would be expected from the Chinese should he be invited to visit your home. Gifts should never be opened in the presence of the donor, as this is considered impolite. The Chinese appreciate sincere compliments; the expression of their appreciation is to deny the compliment.

- Sending white flowers for a happy occasion should be avoided, as white is the colour of sorrow. The same applies to clothes. Red is the most appropriate colour.
- Belching is an expression of well-being and should not be looked upon as ill-mannered.
- Chinese will not accept an invitation to a social event while in

mourning, and will consider it an insult if you ask, should you know the circumstances.

- An appropriate wedding present in Hong Kong is money presented in the form of a gift cheque.
- The Chinese admire Western technology and value education highly. These are subjects of great interest and the Chinese will discuss them readily.

It is best not to use your hands much. Instead of shaking hands, a bow or a nod with a smile is the preferred greeting. If you are not sure exactly what the meaning of a particular gesture is to a Chinese, do not use it. Blinking the eyes at someone is impolite. Pointing should be with the open hand rather than the index finger. Never call someone with the movement of a crooked finger as this is considered very rude. The Chinese beckons someone to come by stretching out the hand and moving the palm downward and inward in repeated movements. This is often confused with the Western good-bye signal.

In Asia, the head, as the resting place of the soul, is the most respected part of the body. The feet play the opposite role. It is impolite to point your feet at someone when crossing your legs. The safest sitting position is with your feet flat on the floor.

The Chinese businessman's wardrobe is conservative. Older businessmen wear dark suits with ties all the year round. Despite the availability of fine tailors and a recent trend in the Hong Kong clothing manufacturing industry towards designer-type clothing, the suggested suit for business is the dark blue or grey suit with a white shirt and an expensive tie. Accessories will be noticed, especially watches and rings.

Women dress slightly more casually than men; it is acceptable to wear sleeveless dresses and trouser suits. However, in the business districts, as in shopping districts, casual clothing (e.g., shorts) is inappropriate for men and women.

The Western and Chinese concepts of who constitutes a friend are very different. For the Chinese, friendships develop only through years of growing up and attending school together. Friends will do almost anything, including lending large sums of money and aiding the family should illness or misfortune strike.

Of pre-eminent importance to the Chinese is the family. The extended family is dominant and filial piety is the great virtue.

Hong Kong is a truly cosmopolitan city as far as restaurants are concerned, with almost all nations represented. There are many Chinese restaurants, with varied types of cuisines:

1. Cantonese: Delicately seasoned, less spicy. Hong Kong is the real home of Cantonese food.
2. Sechuan: Spicy, hot, uses red chilli in many dishes.
3. Peking: Many great cold food and noodle dishes. Also many types of deep-fried foods.
4. Shanghai: Rich, strong scent with ginger used often.

Larger restaurants have English menus and may be more suitable for the inexperienced traveller, but they will probably be more expensive.

The most useful and important business accessory in Asia is the business card. Most cards are printed with Chinese on one side and English on the other. A very useful tip if time is not a problem is to have someone who knows the Chinese language well choose the characters used to represent your and your company's names. A good translation can have a beneficial effect in business dealings, especially with older and non English-speaking businessmen.

Holidays are plentiful, owing to the celebration of both Christian and Chinese holidays. The favourite holiday is the Chinese New Year. During this time, it is customary for all employees to receive an extra month's salary as a bonus. Most employers take their holidays during this time, when almost all of Hong Kong comes to a virtual standstill.

Should formal negotiations be necessary before establishing a business relationship, the following general guidelines are recommended by seasoned businessmen:

- Choose senior people for the team;
- Make sure they have technical and commercial expertise;
- Empower them to make decisions on the spot;
- Be sure the members approach the talks as a team.

Tea is usually served during business meetings, but it will not be touched until *after the host begins.* If the host drinks his tea early in the meeting, it is permissible to follow his lead.

Bargaining is not practised in any of the major stores where prices are clearly marked. However, it is expected in small shops and bazaars. In fact, most merchants are quite proud of their bargaining abilities. On most items the price asked is 30 to 40% above the price you would pay if you bargained; in the case of jewellery it is 50%. Bargaining is a game and if one is in a hurry (the merchants are never in a hurry), or shows anger, or loses one's sense of humour, the game is over. Bargaining is one of the fine arts of the Hong Kong Chinese.

The basic monetary unit is the Hong Kong dollar. All prices and quotations will be in Hong Kong dollars and the businessman should quickly become accustomed to thinking and pricing in those terms. The currency comes in HK$1,000, HK$500, HK$100, HK$50, HK$5, and HK$1 notes and 50, 20, 10, and 5 cent coins. Convertibility is unrestricted and quite convenient as licensed money changers are easily found throughout the city.

There are no currency restrictions or limits on money going into or coming out of Hong Kong. Travellers' Cheques and all major credit cards are used extensively in the Colony.

Historical Context

Hong Kong is composed of three distinct areas, each of which became British territory as a result of different historical events. Hong Kong Island and the Kowloon Peninsula were ceded to the British in 1842 and 1860 respectively as a result of China's losses in the opium wars. The New Territories were leased from China for 99 years, beginning in 1898, and the lease on the New Territories is due to expire in 1997. Following the Sino-British agreement, the whole of Hong Kong will be handed back to China in 1997 and China has committed itself to preserving the present system for fifty years thereafter. While business confidence remains high, personal disquiet has led to a growing exodus of the highly educated in search of an alternative nationality.

The population is estimated at 5.6 million. Large population increases resulted from refugee inflows from China during the Communist Revolution (1949-50), the Cultural Revolution (1967-1968) and the Vietnam War (1978). Chinese make up 98% of Hong Kong's populations, with the largest proportion of that group being of Cantonese origin. Other substantial ethnic Chinese groups are Fukkien, Shanghainese and the Hakka.

Hong Kong Island comprises 29 square miles. Kowloon, situated on the mainland, measures only 3 square miles, but the New Territories, which include all outlying islands, have a land area of 365 square miles. The Central District, on Hong Kong Island, is the main business and financial area of the Colony. Kowloon, which has one of the highest population densities of the world, contains residential and industrial areas, Kai Tak airport, shops, hotels and major shipping wharves. The New Territories are rural, with most of the land used for small farms and rice paddies.

Hong Kong has one of the highest standards of living in all Southeast Asia. However, because of the continuous influx of refugees from China, there is also great poverty.

The Colony functions as a free economy, with minimum interference from Britain. There are very low taxes, almost no import duties or restrictions, and capital and currency flow freely. Hong Kong is said to have more banks than any city in the world and much money is funnelled through the city to the People's Republic of China by overseas Chinese.

Demographic movement
Hong Kong has been experiencing a shift of population from the overcrowded central urban areas outwards. Most of this movement has been into New Kowloon and the New Territories. Over the last 10 years the average age of the population has increased dramatically. Twenty-three per cent of the population was under 15 in 1985, compared with almost 33% in 1975.

The climate is subtropical, and the year is divided between a hot humid summer and a cool — even chilly at times — dry and sunny winter. There are short spring and autumn seasons. Rain, which can be very heavy, falls mainly in spring and summer. There is little difference between day and night temperatures.

Temperatures during the summer range from 25°C (77°F) to 31°C (87°F). The humidity, often 90%, makes summers tiring. Typhoons generally strike Hong Kong between May and November.

In winter, temperatures are moderate — they seldom fall below 10°C (50°F) and can go as high as 20°C (68°F).

The best weather in Hong Kong is in late autumn and early

winter — October and November. In February and March the weather turns wet and misty. Summer begins in May.

Families in Hong Kong are generally large, and in the past it was common for the extended family — grandparents, relatives — to live under the same roof. The large cost of accommodation and small size of flats has resulted in a shift to nuclear families. While there is little display of affection, there is a deep-rooted sense of family unity and obligation. The actions of the individual reflect on the family, so within the family and outside it, Chinese strive for harmony and to avoid loss of face.

Both English and Chinese are used in Hong Kong. The Chinese spoken is the Cantonese dialect of southern China in the nearby Kwangtung Province and Canton. Cantonese is a tonal, monosyllabic dialect that is difficult for Westerners to learn because the different tones are so difficult to pronounce. Cantonese sounds rather gruff to the Western ear, and speakers generally appear to be talking slightly louder than one does in English.

Hong Kong's government structure is unique. Some have called it a relic of 19th-century European colonialism, but it continues to function efficiently. The head of the non-elected government is the Governor, who is appointed by the Queen of England and serves for an average of four years. He is advised by an Executive Council (Exco), which has 15 appointed members.

The Legislative Council (Legco) is responsible for approving and amending all bills and policy decisions, including the Colony's budget. It has 56 members, 24 of whom are elected and the remainder appointed by the Governor or the Queen.

The Urban Council is the only official body with elected members. It has 12 members chosen at district elections and 12 members appointed by the Governor. It is responsible for public health management and control of City Hall, sports and the arts.

The Government Secretariat is the administrative arm of the government. All government departments, such as security and social services, the civil service, and housing, receive their directions from the secretariat.

The system of justice is independent of the government and ranges from the court of appeals to the small claims court, although judges are appointed by the Governor.

The United Kingdom retains total governmental control, but trade matters are generally decided locally. Therefore, local government's non-restrictive attitude to trade has a greater impact than one might imagine.

The Chinese have the reputation of being a hard-working people with a strong sense of family responsibility. This stems from long-held beliefs that originated from the great teacher Confucius and were passed down through centuries by the teachings of his disciples. In Hong Kong, a curious mixture of East and West exists side by side. The Catholic and Protestant religions have the most followers and are the most visible. However, Buddhist temples are plentiful and the family ancestral shrine is present in a great number of homes. This results in an unusual synthesis of culture and religion in which the Western ideas of morality are often brought home by quoting Eastern thinkers.

Many colourful gods, ranging from a sea goddess to a god of the kitchen, are worshipped by the Chinese, who therefore appear to Westerners to be very superstitious. Some of these superstitions carry over into everyday business practices.

The economy

When examining the present structure of business in Hong Kong, the aims of both the United Kingdom and the People's Republic of China must be taken into consideration. Britain needs the trade, while China sees Hong Kong as a window on the rest of the world and a major source of foreign exchange.

Hong Kong's industry can be divided into three sections: manufacturing, light industries and banking. Since the migration from Shanghai in 1947, and the resulting transfer of industrial technology, manufacturing, especially of consumer goods, has increased significantly.

However, with some of the new export restrictions placed upon Hong Kong by the United States and other industrialized nations, exports are likely to drop. The government is now shifting its emphasis to light industries, which are expected to contribute to Hong Kong's strong trade position in the future.

Over 100 licensed banks, with over a thousand branches; more than 2,000 finance companies; 270 international insurance companies; and a thriving market testify to the level of financial activity in Hong Kong, which is one of the busiest trading centres in the world. Hongs, the Chinese word for the large trading houses, are credited with being mainly responsible for the Colony's existence. They date from the 19th century and continue to be strong today. A large number of British, U.S., Australian, Dutch and other countries' companies are located in Hong Kong, as well as many of China's state-owned trading houses.

The Colony's biggest trading partners are the United Kingdom, the United States, and West Germany for its exports, while it imports most from Japan, the United States and China, on whom it relies heavily for food and water, in return for which China receives much of its foreign exchange.

The economic health of the Colony is dependent on outside forces and therefore reflects the economic health of the rest of the world. But if something negative happens, the Chinese have a remarkable ability to adapt their methods to the circumstances and overcome the difficulty, whatever it is.

Hong Kong is a member of the General Agreement on Tariffs and Trade (GATT) and formally pursues liberal trade policies. All preferential treatment for the British Commonwealth was abandoned in 1975 and discrimination against Hong Kong is viewed in the Colony with "concern and disgust".

Through its Department of Commerce and Industry, Hong Kong now negotiates with its trading partners directly rather than through the British government, which, however, still functions as an adviser.

Hong Kong is extremely dependent on foreign trade (80% of GDP consists of merchandise exports), and is therefore vulnerable to fluctuations in the world economy. Even so, despite recent worldwide recessionary trends and growing protectionism in the West, it has fared well because of its strong financial centre and increased trade with China.

The United States is Hong Kong's largest trade partner, with good prospects for U.S. sales of electronic components, industrial equipment, building supplies and equipment, fabrics, consumer goods, computers, fruit, vegetables and foodstuffs. Prospects for re-exports to China are also favourable.

The Colony's main exports are garments (35%), watches, electrical machinery, footwear and plastics, but it is trying to diversify by moving towards the export of more sophisticated manufactured goods.

It is also a good place for investment. There are no exchange controls, low taxes and a good communications network. Trade is virtually free, which makes for stiff competition, but there are nearly no export-import restrictions. The only significant tariffs are on tobacco, liquor and hydrocarbon oils. Because of its relations with China, Hong Kong serves as an excellent base from which to penetrate the Chinese market.

The hustle and bustle seen in Hong Kong are directly related to business — the sole reason for Hong Kong's success and the sole hope for continued prosperity. The economic structure bears perhaps the closest resemblance to a pure free market in the world today. It has been hailed by Milton Friedman and other economists as the prime example of what a totally "capitalist" economy can accomplish, and it has the third highest standard of living in Asia, while managing to absorb over 3 million refugees.

Hong Kong's future looks well planned. Business relations with China have increased dramatically. In fact, the main growth in Hong Kong's exports and foreign trade has come from re-exports and exports to China, as well as increased Chinese investment in the Colony. Businessmen are approaching 1997 with cautious optimism.

Hong Kong will be a service base for China's offshore oil exploration project and will provide supplies, financial support, communications and banking services. China wants and needs Hong Kong's services and technological skills. It is estimated that China will keep the status quo when the lease expires. Hong Kong provides needed access to world markets for China as well as serving as an international financial centre.

Hong Kong's financial services network and banking system are third in the world, after New York and London. Its power as a major financial centre should increase because of new tax concessions, including the elimination of tax on interest on foreign currency deposits in commercial banks.

The economy has remained strong. During the 1970s it averaged growth rates of 11% per annum with average rates of inflation of only 5%. Since then it has slowed down somewhat.

Hong Kong lacks indigenous fuel supplies and imports all its oil requirements. The bulk of the electricity requirements is supplied by two private companies — the China Lights and Power Co., Ltd. and the Hong Kong Electric Co., Ltd. However, Hong Kong and China have initiated a joint venture for the development of a nuclear power plant at Daya Bay in China's Guangdong province. Once completed in 1991, this plant should supply 15-20% of Hong Kong's electricity needs.

The government has traditionally maintained a low profile in the economy. The public sector accounts for only 20% of the GNP. Taxes are low; the standard rate is around 16-17% and 40% of government revenues comes from direct and indirect taxation. The remaining revenues stem from government land and property transactions. The largest expenditures are for building and construction on housing and infrastructure. Social and community services, defence, education and law and order expenses make up the remaining costs.

There is little bureaucracy, and the government believes in minimal interference with the private sector. Regulations govern the registration and operation of companies, and safety and fire provisions in manufacturing establishments. Copyrights and trademarks are protected, as are immigration requirements. Specific regulations cover taxation, which is traditionally lower than in any Southeast Asian country.

Bibliography

Business Strategies for the People's Republic of China. Hong Kong: Business International, Asia Pacific 1980.

Update: Hong Kong. New York: Overseas Briefing Associates, 1978.

Language Research Center, *Culturegram: Hong Kong* Provo, Utah: Brigham Young University, 1979.

Investing, Licensing and Trading Conditions Abroad: Hong Kong. Business International Corp., 1980.

Hong Kong 1978, Ed. by Phillip Rees, Government Information Service, 1978, J. R. Lee, Government Printer.

Edelstein Shirlee, editor, *Living in Hong Kong*, AMCHAM Publications, Hong Kong Ltd. 1977.

Kay, Michele, *Doing Business in Hong Kong*, South China Morning Post Ltd. 1976.

Economic Intelligence Unit, Hong Kong, Macau, Country Profile 1986-87.

INDIA

The exasperating paradise

India has been described as fascinating, preposterous, shocking, elusive, sprawling and exasperating. The late Prime Minister, Indira Gandhi, once said: "India is large, very large and not at all easy to understand. The vastness and complexity could only be comprehended with the aid of compassion and some humour and much patience... If you wish to know something about India, you must empty your mind of all preconceived notions. Why be imprisoned by the limited vision of the prejudiced? Do not try to compare. India is different and, exasperating as it may seem, would like to remain so...This is the secret of India, the acceptance of life in all its fullness, the good and the evil".

Family and friends have an importance far beyond that to which the West is accustomed. A friend's role is to "sense" a person's need and to do something about it. To speak one's mind is a sign of friendship.

Most Indians are fatalistic, which makes them highly resilient, on the one hand, and ready to compromise on the other.

Astrologers play an important role in India, as the people believe that nothing is accidental in the universe. They decide the time for sinking wells, erecting buildings, marrying and other important matters.

Business is based on personal contacts and it is crucial to know the right person in order to get contracts. Corruption, bribes or payments for "fixing" are part of everyday life and must be accepted to get things accomplished.

During your first business meeting with an Indian, general issues should be talked about and a relaxed but formal approach should be adopted towards the relationship. A high pressure approach is usually not successful and a low-key presentation is far better received. Tea or coffee is usually served at business meetings.

Meetings should be planned and appointments should be kept punctually. Foreign businessmen visiting India are likely to be offered lavish hospitality by their counterparts.

For business purposes it is advisable to give small presents to people who have provided assistance, or to those whose interest is to be cultivated.

Usually some time is spent on small talk before getting down to serious business. If the businessman is already known to the visitor, it is appropriate to ask about his family and business associates. The weather, traffic and one's trip are among the topics with which one can start a conversation; to be avoided are comments on smells, poverty or filth. Later, one can discuss philosophical matters, which are relished by Indians, as are cricket, hockey and soccer. And if the visitor can express appreciation of Indian culture, customs and food he will win friends.

Polite diplomacy

Indian businessmen may not always reply with a straight "yes" or "no" to questions. One must be tactful to elicit answers. And it is not advisable to give a blunt refusal to a particular proposal. Polite diplomacy is more effective.

The method of greeting depends upon the social status of the persons meeting. A Western businessman will be considered an equal and as such may use the Indian salutation, *namaste*, meaning "greetings to you" with the palms together in front of the chest.

Among Western educated businessmen shaking hands is entirely acceptable, although it should be avoided with women.

While on a business visit to India it is better to address people formally and not to use a first name until you are invited to do so. Then it is customary to add the suffix *ji* to the first name, e.g., Ravi (a first name) would become Raviji, or precede the first name with 'Mr.', e.g., Mr. Ravi as a mark of respect.

Hindi and English are the official languages. Fourteen other major regional languages other than Hindi are recognized by the Indian constitution. In addition, there are 250 dialects.

Hindi is spoken by approximately 30% of the population. English is used widely in commerce.

Some of the very basic and common words and phrases of the language are given below.

English	Hindi
Hello (meaning "greetings to you")	*Namaste*
Good morning	*Shubh-prabhat*
Please	*Kripya*
How are you?	*Kaise-hai-aap?*
Thank you	*Dhanyawaad* or *Shukriya*

As for non-verbal communication:
- Grasping one's own ears expresses repentance or sincerity.
- A toss of the head means "yes".
- Beckoning is done with the palm turned down; pointing is often done with the chin.
- Backslapping is not a sign of affection.
- The namaste gesture can be used to signal that you've had enough food.

Depending on the kind of house a businessman is invited to, he should take his shoes off at the door, unless asked to keep them on. Inside the house most Hindus walk barefoot or use indoor footwear.

Indian food varies from province to province. About 50% of Hindus are vegetarians; those who are not are nonetheless prohibited from eating beef (the cow is a sacred animal). In the north, wheat bread forms the principal item of food, whereas in the south, the Maratha states and Bengal, rice is the staple diet.

Among respectable Hindus, alcohol is not drunk at home; only non-alcoholic beverages are served.

Western food is available in all the good hotels. Betel leaf (*pān* in Hindi) is usually taken after a meal to aid the digestion and freshen one's mouth.

Hospitality is universal. The duty of entertaining guests is laid down in the Hindu religion as being of prime importance. A well-mannered Hindu will not eat without asking his guest to join him. One is not required to take any gift if invited for supper but, if one does, it will be accepted graciously.

Do not be surprised if you have your meal only with your business partner and not his whole family. Wives and children usually help from the kitchen to make sure that the guest is treated well.

Table manners

At home, eating without knives, forks and spoons is not uncommon. People eat with their hands. If you are dining with the whole family, wait until everybody is at the table before you start eating. Let the host start and begin when you are asked.

Do not get upset if your host asks you several times to have some more food. Simply refuse politely if you don't want more. It is Indian custom to ask repeatedly to make sure the guest does not get up hungry from the table.

Tea and coffee, which are the last items on the supper menu, are usually served in the living-room after dinner. With dinner you drink water only. You might get betel leaf (*pān*) at the end of supper.

When leaving, do not forget to express appreciation of the hospitality and the delicious food.

The Hindu woman, businesswomen or otherwise, wears a sari and blouse. She is extremely loyal to her sari. While most modernized Hindu men have adopted European dress in their outdoor life, the women have kept the sari.

For Western businessmen visiting India, suit and tie is the proper attire. A light coat may be needed in winter and a raincoat and umbrella in the rainy season. Businesswomen should avoid wearing shorts or revealing dresses in public places.

Some behaviour tips

- Say *namaste* — palms together, nod of the head — to greet people.
- Western men should not touch women, and

public displays of affection are inappropriate.
- The left hand is considered unclean. Use the right hand for eating with the fingers or for giving or accepting things.
- Do not lick postage stamps.
- Do not drink water that has not been boiled or filtered.
- Be on time.
- Eat willingly with your hand if the occasion calls for it.
- Don't ask personal questions until you become close to someone.
- Use titles such as doctor and professor.
- Whistling is considered impolite.
- Use the *namaste* gesture to indicate you've been served enough food.

One important thing to remember: Indians are very tolerant and will accept the fact that you are unfamiliar with their customs and procedures.

Historical Context

The ancient land of India began in prehistoric time. Around 500 B.C., Aryans descended from the North and merged with the native Dravidians to form the basis of classical Indian society. The earliest inhabitants settled along the banks of great rivers. Archaeological discoveries reveal that some 5,000 years ago a high-level civilization flourished in the western and northwestern parts of India.

The 16th century saw the Western European nations establishing trading posts in India. The British were very successful and expanded their influence and power in the subcontinent. After World War I, nationalism grew in India. Mahatma Gandhi organized a series of passive resistance campaigns and civil disobedience to British rule. His activities succeeded and in 1947 the peninsula was divided into Hindu India and Muslim Pakistan amidst much rioting and bloodshed. British rule ended on August 15, 1947. On January 26, 1950, the

Indian constitution was promulgated, and the country became a sovereign democratic republic.

The government owns and runs many enterprises such as the airlines, railways, insurance, power facilities and irrigation projects. It also has control of the production of metals, steel, chemicals and engineering equipment. 85% of the nation's banking assets are government-controlled.

The government of India is based on the British parliamentary system, with a two-chamber legislature and executive and judicial branches. The country is governed by a president, who is advised by a Council of Ministers led by the Prime Minister (appointed by the president.) The Council is responsible to the House of the People, the Lok Sabha, which is elected by universal adult franchise.

The current Prime Minister is Rajiv Gandhi.

The dominant religion in India is Hinduism, which is more than a religion — it is a complete way of life. There are also Muslims, Parsees, Jains, Buddhists, Sikhs, Christians and Jews. Hinduism represents approximately 87% of the population.

India is bounded in the northwest by Pakistan, in the north by China, Tibet, Nepal and Bhutan, in the east by Burma, and in the southeast, south and southwest by the Indian Ocean. It covers 3,288 thousand square kilometres and has a population of over 800 million.

There is not enough work for all the people, so poverty is prevalent. Over the past 20 years, India has implemented intensive population control programmes but none have been successful. The high birth-rate has been attributed to early marriage, the emphasis placed on bearing sons by the Hindu religion, the security of having children to take care of their parents in old age, and the low level of education achieved by the rural masses.

India is rich in coal, hydroelectric power potential, industrial raw materials (iron and manganese), and manpower. There has been economic development in only a few isolated sectors of the economy, and the same is true of India's resources, a disadvantage that many attribute to the constraints of tradition and culture.

Climate and culture contribute to the high incidence of disease and influence the patterns of work. The hot weather season brings constant dust, which results in various infections and eye irritations and also limits outdoor physical activity. Vegetarianism contributes to malnutrition and protein deficiencies. The people have a general syndrome known as "weakness" brought on by their constant exposure to epidemic diseases such as cholera and typhus and by malnutrition.

Hinduism perpetuates the caste system, which rigidly separates the social classes and in which privileges or disadvantages are transmitted by inheritance.

Although the Hindu woman's legal position has greatly improved over the years, she is still bound by ancient traditions of behaviour that emphasize her absolute dedication, submission and obedience to her husband and his wishes. This may not be so strictly adhered to in the big cities and Westernized circles, where numbers of women are increasing in the workforce, especially in the professions and in government.

A woman's status in the household is low until she has given birth to a male child. A girl is seen as a burden and a cause of future debt because of the dowry that has to be paid to the husband's family when she marries.

Business decisions have usually to be made within the context of government controls. The private sector is quicker at arriving at a decision but implementation takes time owing to governmental delays. The public sector is plagued by a bureaucratic style of operation and decision-making is, in many ways, coloured by political considerations.

Agency arrangements may be important in doing business in India with the major private import sectors. Therefore businessmen usually find it advantageous to appoint a local Indian firm as their agent.

Correspondence in English is acceptable, as is trade literature, since in practice it is India's foreign trade language. Advertising, to be effective, must be in Hindi as well as English and the provincial language.

Price should be quoted CIF (cost-insurance-freight) or FOB (free on board), as desired by the customer, and in both the foreign currency and Indian rupees.

The Reserve Bank of India is the country's central bank. It acts as banker to the government, the commercial banks and some of the financial institutions.

Commercial banks may be classified into four categories: 1) The State Bank of India and its subsidiaries; 2) nationalized banks; 3) foreign banks; and 4) non-nationalized Indian scheduled banks.

In terms of business, the public sector banks, namely the State Bank of India and nationalized banks, occupy a dominating position. The State Bank of India is the biggest commercial bank in the country, and it also carries out some of the functions of the Reserve Bank. Some of the larger banks also provide a merchant banking service.

The money supply is managed by the Reserve Bank of India. The unit of currency is the rupee. The banking system is deeply involved in the industrialization of the country through financing of both fixed assets and working capital.

Although foreign trade has become an important part of the Indian economy and now accounts for 15% of the GNP, the government's attitude is generally restrictive. Approval of investment is very selective and is granted case-by-case. The government updates its trading policy annually and the rules governing the issue of import/export licences are strictly enforced.

Licences are issued on a CIF basis, and are usually valid for two years. Few letters of credit or payments are permitted without a licence.

A company contemplating collaboration with an Indian firm on technical projects should be aware that payments are in the form of royalties, which must not exceed 5% of the factory price of the product, and can extend for no more than ten years.

English is the major language, and there is a large pool of managerial, skilled and semi-skilled labour. There are also a good and developed capital market and a large domestic market. Imports include fuel, petroleum (two-thirds of crude oil needs are imported), fertilizers, iron and steel, chemicals, machinery, transportation equipment, instruments, paper and gemstones. Exports include textiles, engineering products, gems, jewellery, tea, iron ore, spices, black pepper, nuts, leather, coffee and software.

The main focus of Indian trade policy is on export promotion and import substitution. Over the years the United States has been the largest supplier to India and, with the United Kingdom and the USSR, one of the largest buyers of Indian exports.

India's gross national product has been rising steadily for several years, while inflation has remained relatively low. Since 1950, the country's economy has been directed by a series of Five-Year Plans that set goals and allocate resources. Some major areas to be addressed are electric power generation, irrigation, gas and oil exploration and production and defence.

Tighter control over the money supply is likely as the government attempts to hold down prices and curb inflation. India's economy is very weather-dependent, as 50% of the country's national income is derived from agriculture and allied activities.

The gross national product per capita rate tends to grow more slowly than the population rate. The going rate of pay (1986-87) is $1.50 per day. The last thing India needs is labour-saving modern equipment, with an adult population of 326 million and an official urban unemployment rate of 15 million.

The industrial economy of India has public and private sectors. The public sector companies are government-run industrial and commercial undertakings, while the private sector is composed of profit-oriented business organizations run increasingly by professional managers. The country has made rapid industrial growth in recent years, the capabilities increasing in almost every sphere of industry. Exports have become much more diversified from just agricultural products to light engineering, textiles, sophisticated equipment and even turnkey projects.

Bibliography

Cormack, Margaret & Kiki Skagen, editors, *Voices From India*. New York: Praeger, 1972.

Doing Business in India; Information Guide, Price Waterhouse 1980. October 1980.

Exporter's Encyclopedia, 1981. Dun & Bradstreet International, New York.

Hindustan Year-Book and Who's Who 1979. Edited by S. Sarkar, M.C. Sarkar & Sons Pvt. Ltd., 19 Bankim Chatterjee Street, Calcutta 700073, India

India; A Reference Annual, 1980. Publications Division, Ministry of Information and Broadcasting, Government of India.

Johnson, D.J. & J.E. Johnson, editors, *Through Indian Eyes*. New York: Praeger, 1974.

Lamb, Beatrice P., *India, A World in Transition*. New York: Praeger, 1974.

Language Research Center, *Culturegram: India*. Provo, Utah: Brigham Young University, 1977.

Moore, Clark B., *India, Yesterday and Today*. New York: Bantam Books, 1970.

Roy, G.C., *Indian Culture*. New Delhi, India: Ajanta Publications, 1976.

Sweeney, Leo, *Republic of India*. Kansas City, MO, 1970.

Thomas, P., *Hindu Religion, Customs and Manners*. D. B. Taraporevala Sons & Co., Ltd., 210 Hornby Rd., Bombay.

U.S. State Department, *Area Handbook for the Republic of India*. Washington, D.C.: U.S. Government Printing Office, 1975.

. *Background Notes on the Republic of India*. Washington, D.C.: U.S. Government Printing Office.

The Statesman Year Book 1986/1987, New York: St. Martin's Press, 1986, 123rd ed.

Sowndon, Sondra, *The Global Edge: How Your Company Can Win in the International Marketplace*. New York: Simon & Schuster, 1986.

INDONESIA

Masters of the indirect

Indonesians' desire for harmony is deep-rooted: they seek to maintain harmonious relationships with nature, the world of the spirit and with their fellow men. Clashes, tension, friction, criticism, arguments and confrontations all disturb them greatly. This is in marked contrast to the common American-European goals of efficiency, progress, profit and speed.

Traditionally, Indonesians accept life as it comes. This acceptance, often described as fatalistic, is not wholly passive but is accompanied by various specific actions that are rooted in ancient beliefs.

Islamic faith permeates Indonesian business and social ethics and values. Indonesian Muslims are relaxed and easygoing. They do not follow the rigorous codes of conduct that exist in Arabic Muslim countries.

The long sweep of Indonesian islands encompasses some 300 different ethnic groups, or *sukus*. Most keep their own cultures, customs, beliefs and social structure. Indonesians have lived with ethnic diversity and have an expression that reflects their attitudes: *Lain padang, lain belalang; lain lubuk, lain ikannja* (other fields, other locusts; other pools, other fish).

The old system of traditional customs is being displaced and merging with Western influences in the cities, but remains quite strong in the outlying areas. Village law, not the Koran, prevails in these areas.

Indonesia has a long tradition of government corruption labelled *pungle* (speed money), the means by which many things are accomplished. Since 1970, the government has spent enormous time and energy in attempting to reduce corruption in high places. A highly publicized clean-up programme known as KOPKAMTIB has been launched. Petty officials and a few governors have been changed but the situation remains largely unchanged.

Indonesians love to bargain. They take pride in this art of negotiation. Few prices are fixed except in the big department stores. While bargaining, remember that time, patience, and good nature are required to be successful. Displays of temper are to be avoided in a land where one is especially careful about being *mulu* (ashamed or embarrassed).

Indonesians are masters of the indirect approach. They always go around a subject before mentioning the key point. This gives both parties time to assess one another. Although it takes a bit more time to draw information obliquely, conversations flow with no sense of pressure.

Indonesians avoid direct negatives and can say "no" in many ways while in fact never saying it. An affirmative "yes, but maybe a little later" means "no". Other equivalents to "no" are:

"I'll consider it."

"I'll call you if I hear anything."

"Come back some other time and we will see."

A definite and final "no", an outright refusal, or a turn-down are all considered counter-productive in Indonesia. Phrases that we commonly use, such as "We can't manage that", or "Our management would never allow that", should be avoided. Instead, say: "We hope we can do that", or "We would like to work that out if we can". Negatives should be phrased in affirmative terms, left hanging in the air and incomplete.

Indonesians maintain a calm manner. Displays of emotion such as raising one's voice are considered offensive, so conversations are normally carried on in a soft tone.

Since names can be difficult to catch, using formal engraved calling cards is a good business practice.

Tea or coffee is served whenever you call on a colleague, and expected whenever you are visited.

Negotiations flow according to an established procedure, and decision-making is generally slower than in the West. When discussions get bogged down, it is important not to show impatience.

"There is tomorrow" sums up the Indonesian view of time. "*Jam Karet*" means "rubber time" and is a phrase expressing how time is flexible, stretches or shrinks. Pressure, hurry and impatience are distasteful to them.

There is a basic feeling that one "tempts the gods" if planning is projected too far into the future. Long-range plans are necessary in the 20th century, but aren't viewed as being safe.

The day begins at sunset rather than midnight. The night of a day therefore precedes the day rather than following it. So Monday night is the evening before Monday.

The Western or Gregorian calendar is employed for secular purposes, while the Muslim calendar is employed for religious purposes.

The rite of greeting

Although hand-shaking has become customary in Jakarta, and among most Westernized Indonesians, on the whole people prefer not to have hand contact with others. It is usually considered impolite to shake hands with Indonesian women.

If you smile, nod and bow, and use the terms of respect, *Ibu*, *Bapak* or *Saudara*, when addressing a woman or a man, you will do well.

When leaving a room it is polite to nod to everyone, apologize for leaving and as far as possible make your exit without turning your back, which is considered impolite. It is offensive to point, or use the left hand.

Many newcomers to Indonesia question a person about his job and interests when they first meet him. It is the Western way of getting to know a new person. This is considered impolite and prying to Indonesians. They prefer to talk in more general terms about such things as books, sports or the city's architecture, but not personal matters until they know each other rather well.

Indonesian employees consider it impolite to question their employers. This means that employers need to be especially careful to explain things carefully.

Indonesian culture places considerable emphasis on displays of mutual respect and courteous behaviour. Some important rules of etiquette include:

Don't rush things: Watch quietly, listen carefully, assume an inconspicuous role until you have a feel for the place and people.

When calling on Indonesians: Drinks will be served. Drinks are not to be touched until your host invites you to drink. The cup or glass should not be emptied. Taking a small sip is considered polite. An empty glass will be immediately refilled as often as it is emptied and the guest will appear greedy and unmannerly. Never refuse being served because that is considered a rebuff.

The left hand is unclean: Only use the right hand in eating, passing things to others, and receiving things (money, food, etc.).

Avoid touching: Never touch a person's head, even a child's. It is thought to be the place where the spirit resides. Backs are private and the hearty clap on the back is not appreciated. Men should avoid touching females, and vice-versa, for any reason.

Public affection: This is considered very *kasar* or unmannerly. Kissing, embracing, hand-holding or putting arms around waists shouldn't be done in public.

Sitting on tables: Sitting or placing your feet on a table is considered very *kasar*.

Watch your feet: According to the Islamic faith, the soles of one's shoes are unclean. It is considered very impolite to show the sole of your foot or point your toe at someone. Therefore, it is best to keep both feet flat on the floor and not cross your legs, to ensure that this never happens.

Pointing: This is considered rude and threatening. If one must point, the thumb should be used.

Who goes first? Men go first, not women, in order of rank or position through a door. The host is always last to sit or eat.

Some more general social tips:
— Avoid talking about local politics, socialism, foreign aid and territorial aspirations.
— Make appointments for all business and government calls.
— Gift-giving is customary. Bring small gifts for government officials, businessmen and their wives.

Indonesia's urban centres are much like any other. Restaurants are commonplace. There are also many street vendors in Indonesian cities. Care should be exercised when purchasing this kind of meal.

When dining in an Indonesian home, certain customs should be observed. For example, try not to refuse anything. It is impolite to begin eating or drinking unless invited to do so by the host. When eating, hands are traditionally kept on the table, not in one's lap. Most Westernized Indonesians eat with cutlery. A spoon is used in the right hand, a fork in the left. If utensils are not provided, it is acceptable to request a spoon and fork. It is considered good manners and traditional to compliment the hostess on the meal.

For the overwhelming majority of Indonesians, the central social institution of life is the family. Their family is a complex organization with many interlocking relationships and loyalties that fulfil many needs and obligations in society. Indonesians are very friendly, although not outgoing. They have a highly developed sense of respect for other people. Joking about individuals in the group is not appreciated, and laughing at another's mistakes is offensive.

Because of the tropical climate (Jakarta temperatures average 82°F or 28°C), business suits are not usually worn. Appropriate dress for business is a white shirt, tie and slacks. A long-sleeved batik is considered "formal" wear for men. The only time a suit would be used would be for visits to senior government officials or heads of diplomatic missions. Women should dress modestly, particularly when visiting temples and in strict Islamic areas (e.g., Northern Sumatra).

National language

Since independence, the national language, Bahasa Indonesia (a form of Malay), has been adopted widely among most ethnic subgroups as the language of all written communication, education, government and business. Today, the Indonesian language is understood in almost all villages, although local languages (Javanese being the most common) are still used in many areas.

Bahasa Indonesia (the official national language) is not difficult to pronounce or learn. Each syllable is said exactly as it is written, and there are no tenses. The form is "go today", "go tomorrow", "go yesterday", using auxiliary words instead of tenses.

Simple courtesy phrases include:

Good morning.	*Selamat pagi.*
Good afternoon.	*Selamat siang.*
Good night.	*Selamat malam.*
Good-bye.	*Selamat tinggal.*
Thank you.	*Terima kasih.*
You're welcome.	*Terima kasih kembali.*
How do you do?	*Apa kabar?*
Quite well, thank you.	*Baik, terima kasih.*
Yes; no.	*Ja; tidak.*
Excuse me.	*Ma'af.*
Can you speak English?	*Dapatkah anda berbahasa Inggris?*
What is your name?	*Siapa nama saudara?*

A wide range of food is available. Rice is basic to most Indonesian diets. Many vegetables and edible plants, as well as virtually every known variety of tropical fruit, abound throughout the archipelago. Coconuts are plentiful and are eaten raw or cooked, combined with other foods in many dishes and sauces, or are grated and prepared as a thick cream. Imported frozen foods are also available, but are expensive and the selection is very limited.

A variety of national foods exists. Some of the more common ones are:

Rijsttafel: A smorgasbord of meats, fish, vegetables and curries.

Satay: Beef, chicken, prawns or fish, marinated and then barbecued on split sticks.

Nasi goreng: Rice, fried in coconut oil with eggs, meat, cucumbers, tomatoes and chillies.

Pempek: Delectable fried fish prepared with flour, served in vinegar and dried shrimp sauce.

Gado-Gado: Vegetable salad with spicy peanut dressing.

Soto: Soup with dumplings, chicken and vegetables.

The weather is rarely extreme, but the humidity is usually high. Jakarta is hotter and more unpleasant than Yogyakarta and Denpasar. Nights in Jakarta remain warm, but in Bali, a sea breeze often keeps the heat from becoming oppressive. Dry and wet seasons alternate. In Java, the dry season is from June to

September. In east Java, it lasts from May to October. The dry season is more pleasant.

Historical Context

Indonesia is a grouping of 13,677 islands scattered between Asia and Australia. It is the largest archipelago in the world, extending 3,330 miles east to west, and 1,300 miles north to south. The four main groupings are the Greater Sunda Islands, composed of Java, with a population of 100 million; Sumatra, the sixth largest island in the world with a population of 33 million; and two other large islands. The other three groups of islands include the Lesser Sunda Islands, the Malukus, and West Irian.

The Indonesians trace their ancestry back many centuries. The "Java man", whose fossilized skull was found on Java, dates back 500,000 years. Marco Polo passed through the area in the 13th century, followed by Vasco da Gama in the 15th century, drawing many Europeans to the region in search of wealth. By the 18th century the Dutch had established a monopoly in trade in the Malukus and a dominant position in Java. In 1799 the Dutch government assumed control of Java and embarked on an active policy to exploit the island's natural resources. The introduction of the system of forced labour and the erosion of the traditional social structure provoked deep resentment which by the early 20th century had taken form in the nationalist movement.

Known as the Dutch East Indies, Indonesia remained the territory of the Netherlands until 1942, when it was occupied by the Japanese. Indonesia declared independence in 1945, but the country continued to struggle with intermittent guerrilla warfare until 1949 in order to gain total independence from the Dutch. In 1949, the Dutch transferred sovereignty of nearly all of the land of the Dutch East Indies except West Irian, which joined the republic in 1963. The country became known as the Republic of Indonesia in 1950.

General Suharto has been President of Indonesia since 1966. Suharto's "New Order" remains a strongly centralized government based on the constitution of 1945, which was amended in 1950. Voting is the right of anyone over 17 years of age or anyone who is married, regardless of age.

Indonesia is one of Southeast Asia's most diverse nations — both economically and ethnically. Its population of approximately 175 million, the world's fifth largest, is unevenly distributed. The island of Java, which accounts for 7% of the nation's land mass, houses 63% of the populace.

Although generally of Malay descent, the people of Indonesia have been called the classic example of a plural society. As Indonesia grew as a nation, these regionally ethnic differences persisted and are present today. Thus, the tensions run along ethnic, religious and economic lines.

The labour force of Indonesia is approximately 62.5 million and is growing at about 1-1.5 million per year. Unemployment and underemployment are severe problems, however. The average per capita income is about $530 per year. There is a deepening discontent among many groups of people about differences in living conditions between the very wealthy and the very poor.

Indonesia's populace is about 90 per cent Islamic, although a powerful Christian minority exists. The Muslim majority is a seriously divided one. There are two major groups that have very different spiritual and value orientations: the *abangan* who are nominal Muslims and the *santri* who are devout practitioners.

Religions and loyalties

The *santri* are in turn divided into traditionalists, the majority, and modernists, who believe in a reformed purist Islam and would like to see the establishment of Indonesia as a Muslim state.

These religious differences are clearly delineated, as are the ones between the commercially powerful Chinese minority and the poor Javanese. Yet the conflicts do not divide the nation as a whole. They do, rather, represent a shifting mosaic of cultural and political associations or alliances. In that sense the country's motto of "unity in diversity" is an appropriate description of the modern Indonesian people.

Indonesia is a society where powerful loyalties to tribe and community abound. The communities exert a powerful influence in determining the norms of social behaviour. While the family, as a unit, still dominates the social fabric of the country's rural areas, its pre-eminence has dwindled in the cities. Family ties are still important, but are no longer the overriding concern.

Indonesia's urban centres are generally compartmentalized into ethnic and religious quarters. These neighbourhoods are known as *kampungs*. A *kampung* acts very much like the rural villages, with some actual governmental authority vested in the leadership of each *kampung's* civic association. These neighbourhoods or quarters are not exclusively Indonesian in composition, as there tend to be enclaves of Chinese and other foreign groups.

The social and military élite of Indonesian society live in the large urban areas. Unlike much of the rest of the society, they embrace a rather Western lifestyle. Their way of life forms the heart of the modern and emerging state of Indonesia.

The great body of Indonesians survive by subsistence farming. Their everyday lives are governed by what is known as *adat* — a blend of local law and custom. Heterogeneity is the watch word, as rural Indonesia remains a patchwork of culturally different regions — each characterized by the religious, linguistic, judicial and tribal customs common to the area.

The economy
Since the Suharto government came to power, it has followed a strategy of stabilization, rehabilitation and economic development.

In the 1980s, private and foreign investment were actively sought, especially from Japan and the United States. Capital goods, mining and minerals, light industry, agribusiness, transportation and export industries are targets for investment.

In recent years, Indonesia has been heavily dependent on its oil exports, rising and falling with the fortunes of its fellow OPEC members. Although exports of goods and services in other sectors are expanding, growth is constrained by the limited scope and competitiveness of the country's products. The export of agricultural commodities will probably increase, and other exports are likely to grow from the multimillion-dollar investments in natural gas, nickel and bauxite.

Japan is Indonesia's largest aid donor and accounts for the largest share of total foreign investment and loans.

Major imports of food are still required despite strenuous

efforts and significant investments in agriculture and rural development. The balance of payments remains a major problem. A shrinking merchandise trade surplus, coupled with rising interest payments and other outflows, will continue to widen the current account deficit. Servicing the external debt burden takes 20% of export earnings yearly.

Indonesia's relatively slow economic progress has resulted from complex social, historical and geographical factors, many of which are carry-overs from the colonial period and the struggle for independence. The most identifiable vestiges hampering economic progress have been an inadequate rate of savings, a lack of education and training and a long period of mismanagement and neglect of the economy in the 1950s and 1960s.

With its wealth of natural resources, Indonesia has the potential to be a prosperous nation. Yet with a low per capita income, large population and limited resources in overcrowded Java, it remains a poor country.

Bibliography

Davis, Gloria, *What is Modern Indonesian Culture?*, Athens, Ohio: Ohio University, 1979.

Lanier, Alison R., *Update-Indonesia*. Overseas Briefing Associate, 1978.

McVey, Ruth, *Survey of World Cultures — Indonesia*. Yale University, 1963.

Neill, Wilfred T., *Twentieth-Century Indonesia*. University Press, 1973.

Indonesia — Business Profile Series. The Hong Kong and Shanghai Banking Corporation, 1978.

Vreeland, Nena; Just, Peter; Martindale Kenneth W.; Moeller, Philip W.; Shinn, Rinn-Sup, *Area Handbook for Indonesia;* Third Edition 1975, pages 1-488.

Moran, Robert T., and Harris, Philip R., *Managing Cultural Synergy*, Gulf Publishing Company, 1981.

Foreign Economic Trends (FET), Indonesia. Department of Commerce, January, 1986.

Business International: Asia Pacific Forecasting Services. Indonesia, May 1986.

JAPAN

The endless sunrise

Group consensus is a key attitude in Japanese business, and two very fundamental values rule behaviour. The first is absolute loyalty to the company employer. Work is honourable and a privilege. The second is an overwhelming identification with the place of employment. Japanese are hired at a young age from school and most will remain with the company throughout their lives. A high premium is placed on company loyalty and the team concept. Employees are expected to defer to group over individual interests.

While the overall attitude towards work is very positive and highly disciplined, in recent years there has been a shift away from some traditional values. Japanese are highly competitive and anxious to reach the top managerial jobs where they command a high degree of respect. Among younger employees there has been some dissatisfaction with the traditional promotion by seniority. Nonetheless, Japanese show respect for age and hierarchical position.

Overall, the Japanese value mild, undemonstrative and humble attitudes. They are extremely anxious to avoid unpleasantness or confrontation. The Westerner is well advised to observe these values. "Saving face" is a key concept. The Japanese are extremely sensitive to mutual perceptions of self-esteem.

They learn never to make another person look foolish. They constantly strive to maintain harmony in their relationships even though there are acceptable times and places for disagreement.

Japanese take their identities from their work and companies. Employees owe their company hard work and loyalty, and companies owe their employees employment, benefits and a good image.

Japanese rarely take cases to court as this would imply open conflict and a total breakdown in harmony. When serious complications arise in business, the Japanese prevail upon an arbiter to resolve the difficulty. This arbitration is usually accepted as binding in a court of law.

Government and business representatives tend to work and plan closely together. Objectives are usually formed by the two groups in collaboration. When the government makes a policy statement, business has had a hand in formulating it.

The large trading companies are economic leaders and work directly with the government in setting economic policy. The Bank of Japan reviews the impact of any agreements that might influence the domestic economy. Their evaluation and recommendation are then sent to other concerned government agencies. Government involvement is essential in any major negotiations that affect either the national interest or those of an entire industry.

It is prudent to be aware of appropriate government channels, as the achievement of national objectives is a mutual aim of both business and government. Both the Economic Planning Agency and the Ministry of International Trade and Industry (MITI) establish guidelines for all international transactions. Guidelines are enforced not by the agencies themselves, but by individual agents who act as intermediaries between the public and private sector.

Yet it would be wrong to assume that business and government in Japan have a single compatible goal in mind at all times. Conflict does arise, both within different government ministries, as well as between competing economic sectors. Unlike many Western nations, the Japanese government enjoys a proportionately small ownership of industry. Thus private industry maintains a very powerful voice in Japan's economic direction.

The Japanese use extremely complex and ritualized forms of greetings and leave-takings. The level of formality depends on the situation and persons involved. Nowadays, in business situations, people use the standing bow, often together with a handshake, while saying their greetings and good-byes. The depth of the bow is determined by the overall formality and the status of the persons involved.

It is important to open and close all meetings with some formality. Foreigners are not expected to bow as a Japanese might. The best approach is to wait quietly until the person has been introduced (this may occur standing or sitting), and give a nod of the head as you extend your hand. A nod of the head in place of the bow shows deference and humility (positive traits in Japanese culture).

Business cards are an absolute must for business as well as social situations. These should be printed in both Japanese and English. When meeting someone for the first time, it is customary to give and receive cards. Printed on the business card is the person's rank (title), company and phone number.

Never address a Japanese business contact by his first name. Even close friends in Japan use the last name. If the president of a company says please use my first name, it is his privilege, but it shows your measure of respect to refrain and continue with the last name. Some Westerners feel uncomfortable being called by their last name after they feel some distance has been bridged.

Some sartorial guidelines

While the Japanese are becoming less formal than previously in their office wear, they are still much more conservative than most Westerners. Shirts, ties and jackets are worn for all business calls and luncheons. Dark suits and white shirts are preferred. Patterns are absent or very unobtrusive. Conservative dress is expected for top managerial positions.

Footwear should be chosen so that it can be easily removed for entrance into special places, as dining and other activities may be conducted on tatami floors (straw mats) and clothing should be selected accordingly.

Banks and other financial institutions issue uniforms to women clerks. In fact, business dress, company-issued or not, is like a uniform. Japanese are also highly aware of status symbols in dress, e.g., designer signatures, look of quality, subdued colours, imported goods.

For women, clothing and hairstyles are basically the same as one would wear to a company call in the West. Businesswomen are still uncommon in Japan, and it is even more important to look the part.

Protocol must be scrupulously observed in Japan. Showing the proper deference and respect for others is considered essential, as is expressing your gratefulness for any favours or special attention. Failure to do so may easily result in cancelled negotiations.

Personal relations are a fundamental basis to all Japanese transactions. Business is frequently introduced over tea, *sake*, or a game of golf. This is a time for evaluating each individual's strengths and weaknesses. You are expected to remain polite and respectful, friendly without becoming overly familiar.

Entertaining will continue to be a large part of business. Both top and middle management will want to entertain you over business transactions and you may find yourself beginning negotiations from the start with each new group. Wives are generally not expected to accompany husbands on business/social occasions unless *specifically* invited to do so. This custom is strictly observed.

The art of giving

Giving gifts is expected in Japan. If someone was particularly helpful a gift of Scotch or cognac is in order. If the gift is to a "superior", it must be perceived as valuable so as not to be taken as an insincere gesture. It is best to err on the side of over-generosity. If a business party is held, guests are usually given a gift — specific items may be Scotch, elegant soap packages, confections, flowers, coffee, tea or spices. The gifts should be chosen from a "name" store such as Mitsukoshi or Takashimaya.

Be on time and preferably 10 minutes early for appointments. Japanese try to be on time. If you have an appointment with a senior executive, you will often be taken care of by a junior person while waiting for the executive to make an entrance. Generally, guests, especially first-time guests, are shown into a quiet, tastefully decorated lounge and served Japanese tea, sometimes coffee or juice. Rise when another member enters the room to be introduced.

For ongoing relationships, it is customary to personalize service to clients and associates. Salesmen have even sent gifts to a client's daughter on her birthday because the client's favourite subject was his daughter's achievements. Anything important to the client is important to the supplier, including golf, a favourite whisky brand and holiday plans.

Before the businessman arrives in Japan, appointments should already be scheduled. If a trader has an intermediary in Japan, necessary appointments can be scheduled by this person or organization; alternatively, the services of a securities firm or trading company can be used. The trading companies virtually dominate the import/export dimension of the Japanese economy.

Many customs are based on a traditional sense of respect for age and status, and the male-orientation of Japanese society. Men expect to take precedence over women and do not practise Western customs of rising when introduced to or deferring to women. Older people are revered, and should be allowed to speak first.

Japanese prefer low speaking voices and quiet laughter. Gifts will usually be unopened until the receiver has returned home. The Japanese place great emphasis on giving thanks for all favours or entertainment — a prompt telephone call or note to your hostess is expected.

Learning to use chopsticks is not difficult and shows a sincere interest in the Japanese culture. Never cross chopsticks on your plate, leave them sticking up into food or leave them lying in your ricebowl.

Guests should be treated royally. When you are the guest, be appreciative and recognize all the effort as well as anticipating how you might reciprocate. Show some hesitation in taking food, drink, going first and talking about your achievements.

If you are invited to a private home (a rare occasion) you must respond in kind with a dinner in a private room of the hotel or restaurant.

If sitting on the floor, men can cross their legs and take their jackets off after the toast.

In informal situations the Japanese eat *sushi* with their fingers, although in the posher restaurants chopsticks would be used.

At large formal dinners it is common to sing songs. Everyone should join in, and individuals should have a song ready if asked to perform.

In traditional restaurants, the waitresses often become quite involved in dinner conversation and sometimes they make food at the table.

When one is entertaining at home, a wife does not normally join the guests. She serves food and warms *sake*. This custom varies depending on the purpose and rank of the guests.

The Japanese have developed certain peculiarities in their use of the English language. Here are examples of words that are often misunderstood.

Japanese use "service" to mean something free or at a discount.

Westerners use "deadlines" even when they are not really necessary. Japanese do not use deadlines so much, but when they do, they are serious.

"Guarantee" often means free service, to replace parts within a certain time.

"Yes" often means "I understand" or "I agree"; it can sometimes mean no.

"No" is a strong word. A Japanese may think the Westerner has cut off the deal if he says "no", while in fact he is only disagreeing with one point. It is therefore best avoided; "perhaps" is just as effective and more polite.

Japanese sometimes use words like "problem" when they do not want to say "no".

"I understand" or "I see" can mean "I will carry that out" or "I agree". It can also mean "no".

Conversation should concentrate on points of agreement rather than disagreement. Compromise and harmony are stressed at all times.

The Japanese prefer a calm, unemotional state of mind. Discussing sorrowful subjects is considered in bad taste as it makes the listener unhappy.

It is best to avoid discussing politics until a very good relationship has been established, simply because misunderstandings are easily generated.

Visitors will be asked about their trip over, their impressions of Japan and whether they like Japanese food. Talk about, or *around*, your business, where you usually do business, various countries you have visited. Your contacts in Japan are also topics of conversation. Although Japanese work long hours, they like to talk about hobbies, which can be anything from photography or mountain climbing to Chinese bronze study. Talking about hobbies allows people to get to know one another a little better on a personal basis without invading privacy. It also often leads to discovery of common interests. From there, a discussion of sports, arts, music, Japan's progress, the company's achievements, new products, history or famous people is acceptable.

Men should not be forward with the women in the office beyond being courteous. Women should be careful not to be too aggressive or strident.

Unless contacts have previously been established with the Japanese company, the first appointment should be made with one of the larger trading companies or a securities company. Many Japanese companies deal exclusively through these organizations. The other alternative is finding an appropriate contact or connection who can introduce you to the company and be of assistance should difficulties arise during negotiations. He will then act as an intermediary.

Protocol for meetings
Meetings begin with the formal exchange of business cards. A good rapport should be established before it is appropriate to attach *san* (the general term for Mr./Ms.) after the proper name — such as "Hayakawa san".

Seating is generally arranged so that the most senior manager is in the middle of the group, with the next most senior man to the right and the middle managers on the left. Frequently the first meeting is designed solely to establish an atmosphere of friendliness and harmony. Compliments are exchanged — never jokes. Sincerity is crucial at this stage, as well as humility. Some impersonal gifts may be exchanged.

After the initial meeting, subsequent efforts will be focused on building good relationships rather than immediately specifying the actual contract. Negotiations are normally conducted by several Japanese teams. It is advisable to employ your own translators in order to ensure that communication is as complete as possible.

The spokesman for the Japanese team is not always the leader, but rather the person who speaks English best. The Japanese team members routinely compare notes, draft memos and repeat questions that have already been answered. Several meetings may be called. Throughout this process the Western negotiator should remain patient and sincere — the atmosphere of mutual agreement must be maintained.

A prolonged period of silence, or hesitance in speech, as well as a disinclination to be specific, are all possible indications that negotiations are not going well. An intermediary may be the best solution if negotiations break down.

The decision-making process can be very tedious for the Westerner. The *ringi-sei* system, described in a later section, is time-consuming. The negotiator has little alternative but to await the outcome.

The Japanese generally do not like complicated legal documents. A good compromise is usually a written contract which covers the essential points but still leaves either party room to make adjustments as the need arises. This carries through to implementing the contract — the Japanese expect both parties to be able to alter performance as circumstances change. The Japanese do not feel bound to any written document until they have affixed their seal.

In Japan, politeness at all times is a must. There is no separate business style; formal good manners are the rule for all occasions.

Three levels of formality can be found. The highest level of politeness is maintained between important strangers (as in first business meetings) or when one desires to show extreme respect. A slightly less formal politeness is used for daily interactions among peers, or once negotiations have begun. The least strict formality would be found among friends, or between very top management and those much lower in the hierarchy. It is important to be extremely sensitive to these levels of formality and respond in kind.

Maintaining face — or self-respect — is crucial. Negative responses are avoided at all costs. Japanese prefer to talk around an issue, since getting straight to the point might involve some confrontation.

The Japanese maintain a very clear perception of personal

space — both physically and psychologically. In greeting, that is why the Japanese bow rather than embrace or shake hands. This preserves an actual physical distance. When laughing, the Japanese covers his mouth to show that he is not laughing at someone.

Many Japanese expressions and gestures may seem confusing to the Westerner. When beckoning someone, the Japanese hold their hands palm downward and motion with the fingers. Smiles or laughter are shown equally for happiness, amusement, embarrassment and anger. It is extremely important to be sensitive to the mood and not presuppose meanings based upon what the gesture means in a Western culture.

The Japanese perception of time is much more subjective than it is for a Westerner. Negotiations that might take two days in the United States or Germany will probably take two weeks in Japan. Preliminary negotiations may be very prolonged while the atmosphere and issues are carefully assessed. Not being hasty is seen as a sign of wisdom and sincerity. Frequently top level managers cannot be reached on short notice because they are so involved in meetings and human relations activities.

Yet the Japanese can also be incredibly efficient and aware of critical deadlines, as in production. Here they make no concession to subjective time. They tend to be punctual. If the negotiator is kept waiting for a very long period, he can usually assume that his request has met with disfavour. A delayed response is generally the polite way for a Japanese to say no.

There is always time for courtesy, and time to help a friend or associate, and to repay social favours. Because reciprocity is a rule, people place high priority on these social obligations and niceties.

Getting physical
Foreigners typically experience Japanese as clean, tidy, disciplined, austere and excessively polite — or, in airports and subways, as rude, pushy people who will use knees, elbows and thumbs to force their way from one place to another. These constrasting behaviours arise from the Japanese belief that there are two kinds of people — those who exist and those who don't. If a Japanese has some form of relationship with another person, he

observes clearly defined rules regarding how to act. But for those with whom there is no relationship, anything goes.

The Japanese exist within a hierarchical social system in which obligation and duty to those they know is of paramount importance. The Japanese are acutely sensitive to what other people think, and this concern for face is a major guideline to Japanese behaviour.

The austerity, tension, discipline and control cause tensions that find their outlet in restaurants, bars and cabarets. The Japanese revel in consumer goods and in the material and sensuous aspects of life.

Historical Context

The exact origin of the Japanese people is uncertain, but it is believed they have inhabited their four major islands plus many of the smaller ones for at least 6,000 years. Early Japanese culture was influenced by Buddhist missionaries from China, who contributed to many of the basic assumptions about life. This tradition valued external order and harmony within the society. It also emphasized the collective aspect of the social order.

Prior to the Meiji Restoration in 1868, Japan was isolated for more than 250 years. The social and business system in Japan today is based upon dependence, loyalty, strong group cohesion and family ties. The overall goal for Japanese, in the present as in the past, is harmony with people and nature.

Japan consists of an archipelago of four major islands and thousands of smaller ones. The major cities, Tokyo, Osaka, Kobe and Kyoto, are all located on the largest island — Honshu. Although it is only 120 miles away from the Asian mainland, Japan has maintained an unusual degree of insularity and homogeneity, producing a very formalized culture.

Japan's land area is approximately the size of California, yet only 20% of this mountainous country is arable. The population is around 122 million — the most densely populated major country in the world. Japan must import over 30% of its food supplies, and almost 85% of its energy resources. Yet the average income for a Japanese family, including fringe benefits, has surpassed that of its U.S. counterpart. Japan has achieved almost unprecedented success in economic productivity, educational standards, health and welfare.

Japan's first political party was formed in 1870 and called *Aikoku koto.* It is significant because the party presented a petition to the Emperor to establish a parliamentary form of government.

Currently, there are seven major political parties: The Liberal Democratic Party (LDP), Japan Socialist Party, Komeito (The Clean Government Party), Democratic Socialist Party, Japan Communist Party, New Liberal Party and the United Social Democratic Party.

Japan's constitution went into effect on May 3, 1947, advocating sovereignty, human rights and the renunciation of war. The constitution gives judicial power to the Supreme Court and the executive power of the government is executed by the office of the Prime Minister and cabinet. The Emperor's role has changed drastically. Now powerless in matters of government, the Emperor is a symbol of the state.

The Diet, or Parliament, makes laws, approves the national budget, ratifies treaties and initiates draft amendments to the constitution which are then presented to the people. The Diet has two houses, the House of Councillors (upper house) and the House of Representatives (lower house). The lower house has more power than the upper house since it can pass bills rejected by the upper house with a two-thirds vote.

The Prime Minister is the head of the Cabinet. His duties include supervising the government administration and civil service, presiding at cabinet meetings, representing the cabinet in the Diet, and submitting government proposals to the Diet for approval. The Prime Minister has the power to dissolve the lower house. Cabinet ministers are civilians and most must be Diet members. The Prime Ministers can also dissolve the Diet if necessary.

The Supreme Court consists of 15 justices appointed for life by the Cabinet. The Supreme Court is the highest court for civil and criminal cases. It administers the entire court system.

Although Japan is a predominantly secularized country, most of its people will profess to being either Buddhist or Shinto.

Christianity and other world religions account for only about 2% of the population. Freedom of religion is guaranteed in the Japanese constitution.

Buddhism, transplanted from India in the sixth century, emphasizes quiet introspection and harmony. Its influence can be found in Japan's social mores and customs, as well as in its art, literature, music and architecture.

Shinto is native to Japan and is a symbol of Japanese nationalism. The Shinto influence is seen in the Japanese respect for nature and ancestry, and many of the great traditions in both festivals and holidays are attributed to Shinto.

The latitude of Japan extends approximately from that of central France to North Africa, with similar temperatures and seasons. Rainfall can be substantial — with either very humid or very chilly weather. Most Japanese buildings are air-conditioned.

The economy

Japan is the largest industrial and consumer market in Asia as well as the third largest market of all nations. At first, Japan seems like many markets in the industrialized world. Novice traders are often impressed with similarities in business systems and minimize important differences. To seasoned Western traders, working in Japan is sometimes frustrating. But, with patience, an understanding of the Japanese mentality and business system, as well as good business acumen, working with the Japanese can be both challenging and rewarding as well as highly profitable.

International trade in Japan is dominated by trading companies, or *shosha*. Ten companies out of over 5,000 handle 5% of Japan's exports and 60% of its imports. Mitsubishi and Mitsui are two of the largest. The trading company is frequently a complete organization, providing functions from manufacturing to marketing to distribution, and may even go so far as to include banking facilities.

The basis of the Japanese economy is still the small and medium-sized firm, which accounts for over half the nation's workforce. They are the sub-contractors for the giant trading companies.

The consumer market in Japan is greater than the total oil revenues of all OPEC members together. The outlook for continued growth in Japan is positive.

Japan's basic imports are food, minerals, and oil. Because it has a very poor natural resource base, the country imports most of its energy needs. Major efforts have been made in recent years to reduce energy dependence, especially through the development of hydroelectric, geothermal, solar and nuclear power sources. Japan now represents the world's fourth largest country in nuclear power generation capacity.

Japan is a land that has survived and grown on the basis of foreign trade. The economy has until recently expanded through export earnings and high degrees of personal savings and private investment. Increasing world protectionism against Japanese exports and very high oil prices have slowed down growth due to trade.

When oil prices rose dramatically in 1980, labour productivity rose even more than wage increases, preventing inflation from going any higher than 8% during that year. Labour productivity, still growing at a faster pace than wage increases, helps to control inflation.

Japan's principal postwar industries are iron and steel, petrochemicals, electric home appliances and automobiles. Major growth areas will be process industries and electronics technology, particularly integrated circuits, as well as finance and service-related areas. In terms of exports and imports, Japan is becoming a more sophisticated market. Coking coal, logs and lumber traditionally lead U.S. exports to Japan. Industrial products include computer technology and software, food processing and packaging, laser technology and aircraft. The steady increase in Japan's consumer needs is favourable to Western manufacturers.

The Economic Planning Agency is primarily responsible for providing guidelines for balancing national development. The Ministry of International Trade and Industry (MITI) encourages modernization by establishing a fast pace and high standards for all industries. MITI policy generally seeks to guide resources into those areas of production where Japan can compete best internationally. Recently Japan has begun to concentrate heavily on service and knowledge-intensive industries as its energy costs for production have skyrocketed.

Bibliography

Harris, Philip R. and Robert T. Moran, *Managing Cultural Differences*. Houston, Texas: Gulf Publishing Company, 1988.

Miller, Roy Andrew, *Japanese Language in Contemporary Japan*. Washington, D.C.: American Enterprise Institute for Public Policy Research, 1977.

Shigeo, Ozaki, *America-jin to Nippon-jin* (Americans and Japanese). Tokyo: Kodansha, 1980.

Takeuchi, Hiroshi, *Minzoku to Fudo no Keizai-gaku* (Economics of Peoples and Climate). Tokyo: Toyokeizaisha, 1981.

Tyler, V. Lynn et al., *Reading Between the Lines: Language Indicators Project*. Provo, Utah: Eyring Research Institute, 1978.

Reischauer, Edwin O., *The Japanese*. Tokyo: Charles E. Tuttle Co., 1978.

Galante, Steve, "Secrets of Japanese Managers' Success". *Asian Wall Street Journal,* June 29, 1981, p. 11.

Yang, Charles Y, "Management Styles: American Vis-a-Vis Japan". *Columbia Journal of World Business,* Autumn 1977, pp. 23-30.

Mino, Hokaji, "Cultural Differences Create Enigma Image". *Business Japan,* September 1980, pp. 29-33.

Vogel, Ezra F., *Japan as Number One*. Cambridge: Harvard University Press, 1979.

Sekiguchi, Sueo, *Japanese Direct Foreign Investment*. Allanheld, Osmun and Co. Publishers, Inc., 1979.

Menzies, Hugh D., "Can the Twain Meet at Mitsubishi?". *Fortune,* Time Inc., Los Angeles, California, January 26, 1981.

Ouchi, William, *Theory Z., How American Business Can Meet the Japanese Challenge*. Reading, Massachusetts: Addison-Wesley Publishing Co., 1981.

Moran, Robert T., *Getting Your Yen's Worth: How to Negotiate with Japan Inc*. Houston, Texas: Gulf Publishing Co., 1987.

Baldwin, Frank, editor, *From Politics to Lifestyles: Japan in Print, II*. (East Asia Papers: No.42), Cornell: China-Japan Pgm., 1986.

Mitsubishi, staff, *Tatamae & Honne: Good Form & Real Intention in Japanese Business Culture*. Free Press, New York, 1987.

Morton, W. Scott, *Japan: Its History & Culture*. McGraw-Hill, 1984.

Ishida, Takeshi, *Japanese Political Culture: Change & Continuity*. Transaction Books, 1983.

Bowring, R. J., *Mori Ogai & the Modernization of Japanese Culture*. (Oriental Publication Ser.: No.28), Cambridge University Press, 1979.

Okimoto, Daniel I. & Rohlen, Thomas P., editors, *Inside the Japanese System: Readings on Contemporary Society and Political Economy*. Stanford University Press, 1987.

Dower, John W., *Japanese History and Culture: Seven Basic Bibliographies*. Wiener Pub. Inc., 1986.

Hayashi, Shuji, *Culture & Management in Japan*. Columbia University Press, 1986.

Ozaki, Robert S., *The Japanese: A Cultural Portrait*. C.E. Tuttle, 1978.

Varley, H. Paul. *Japanese Culture*, 3rd edition. U.H. Press, 1984.

MALAYSIA

A taste of tradition

Courtesy, etiquette, gentleness and good manners have traditionally been marks of Malay culture, and these values have remained intact despite modernization and urbanization.

A fundamental concept surrounding the Malay ethical system is *berbudi*. The basis of *berbudi* is respect and courtesy, especially towards elders, affection and love for one's parents, a pleasant disposition, harmony in the family, the neighbourhood and in society as a whole. There are two forms of *berbudi*. The first is *adab*, which means that the individual has a responsibility to show courtesy at all times. The second form is *rukun*, which means that the individual must act in such a way as to foster harmony in the family and/or society.

Malays generally do not value the pursuit of wealth for its own sake. Life is viewed as a passing thing, and family or friends take precedence over such selfish interests as the accumulation of profit and other materialistic objectives.

The Malays have a deep respect for traditional customs, even though these customs sometimes conflict with their religion. In these instances, the main Malaysian religion, Islam, has been adapted to fit more effectively with the traditional customs. Such traditional practices and/or beliefs are called *adat,* the Malay word for "custom". The importance of these *adat* is illustrated by their proverb: "Let the child perish but not the *adat.*"

Man is considered basically good by the Malay. Due to his grounding in Islamic faith, the Malay looks upon man as being in harmony with nature. At times the Malay feels subject to the elements, revealing a fatalistic attitude and his belief in the supremacy of God's will. On the other hand, the Malay believes he is part of the natural world and that that world can be perceived animistically — the belief that not only animals but plants as well have a spiritual dimension.

The Malay pays little attention to what has happened in the past, and regards the future as both vague and unpredictable. Planning for the future and/or hoping that the future will be better than either the present or the past is simply not his way of life. This is in contrast to the high value Westerners tend to place upon the future and planning for its arrival.

Individual talents and characteristics are held in high esteem in the West, but the Malay places more significance on interpersonal relationships with relatives, friends and colleagues.

Trust: the top priority

Trust is also a key consideration for the Malay, for it is fundamental to the development of successful interpersonal relationships. A person's capability for loyalty, commitment, and companionship are the key characteristics by which the Malay generally bases his trust.

For the Malay, the process of developing trust is a gradual one. It grows over the course of an association, and is not based upon the professional accomplishments of the individual.

Malays show respect initially through formalities. As a relationship progresses, however, formalities are slowly dropped until an informal atmosphere is achieved. Malays respect the person who shows that he is willing to give and take as the situation may require, unlike many Westerners who attribute respect to one who is aggressive and demonstrates that he can achieve what he wants. The one who compromises is the one to be most respected, for he has developed understanding and empathy for the other's viewpoint. As a result, in negotiations the skilful compromiser will often receive much more than he ever anticipated.

When the Malay meets a stranger, he not only evaluates the person but also his background, family and social position. Whereas in the West one's status is based more upon what one has done, in Malaysia, status is based upon who one is. Indeed, in Malaysia the process by which one attained status in business, government or in other institutions was mainly through birth or social position. High-born people are expected to demonstrate leadership. A leader is also expected to be devoutly religious, humble, sincere, and tactful. The Malay is attuned to viewing society in hierarchical terms, as having a structure with clearly defined roles for persons at different levels, with emphasis placed, nonetheless, upon growth in interpersonal relationships.

Work is viewed by the Malay as but one of many activities in life. Throughout his life he spends a large percentage of his time developing deeper relationships with family and friends. Youth as well as old age are revered in the work place as well. Older persons are revered as advisers and counsellors to the younger workers.

When a Malay receives a promotion, it is as a consequence of his superior's respect and high regard for him. It is not so much a function of his performance in quantitative terms, as would be the case in the West.

Decision-making is generally top down, authoritative, subjective, intuitive, concerned with conserving existing interpersonal relationships.

Decision-making depends a great deal on the Malay becoming personally familiar with his counterpart in negotiations. Without the establishment of such familiarity (i.e., trust in the other's sincerity more than in his technical expertise), decision-making can be forestalled for quite some time if not utterly precluded. Malaysians of Chinese or Indian origins do not fit these rigorous patterns.

Most Malaysians are bilingual and many are multi-lingual. Apart from the national language — Bahasa Malaysia — and such languages as Chinese and Tamil, about half of all Malaysians can speak and write English, the language of commerce. Government policy decreed in 1983 that the language of instruction in schools of all levels will be Malay.

The literacy rate is about 25% in East Malaysia and over 50% in West Malaysia. Bahasa Malaysia is the official language of West Malaysia (from 1967) and Sabah (from 1974) and both English and Bahasa Malaysia are the official languages of Sarawak.

Bahasa Malaysia has an extensive vocabulary of loan words from Sanskrit, Arabic, and English. Five different styles or modes of speech are used: standing, trade or bazaar, court, traditional literary and modern literary. The Dewan Bahasa dan Pustaka (State Office for Language and Books) was established in 1959 to develop and enrich the language.

The Chinese speak nine distinct languages and Indians speak one of about seven languages.

Despite government efforts to promote the use of Bahasa, English is the language of the educated elite and is almost exclusively used in courts and commerce. English is a compulsory second language in all schools beginning with the primary grades.

A Malaysian Language Lesson — Helpful Phrases

Good morning	Selamat Pagi (sah-lah-maht pah-gee)
Please	Silakan (see-la-kan)
Thank you	Terima kasih (t'ree-mah kah-seeh)
Yes	Ia (yah)
No	Tidak (tee-dak)
I don't understand	Saja tidak faham (sah-yah tee-dak fa-ham)
Yesterday	Kemaren (kah-mah rehn)
Today	Hari ini (hah-ree ee-nee)
Tomorrow	Besok (bess-oak)

Like many Asian nations, the concept of time in Malaysia is polychronic — i.e., of a circular, not linear, nature. In contrast to the Western tendency to consider time in a monochronic fashion (time is linear, time is a straight line with a past, present and future), the Malay believes that everything in life must be dealt with in terms of its own time. For a Malay, time is circular. Objects and experiences within time are ever-recurring, cyclical, never ending. One can never be without time because it is infinite. Indeed, one does not have to worry about there not being enough time nor of wasting it, for such ideas are not consistent with the Malay's conception of time nor with his behaviour "within" it.

In the Malaysian cultural milieu there are three ethnic groups: the Malay or *bumiputra* (i.e., "sons of the soil"), the Chinese, and the Indian. Ethnic stereotypes persist among the groups.

Indians and Chinese tend to view Malays as indolent, disorganized, and untidy, though maintaining high standards of personal cleanliness. Malays are also viewed as headstrong, erratic, and quick to take offence. Chinese are convinced that Malay poverty is a consequence of thriftlessness and a distaste for hard work, and that their own economic success results from hard work, thrift, and adaptability. In a more positive vein, Malays are seen as loyal, polite, and as taking pride in their personal appearance.

On the other hand, the Chinese are thought by the Malays and Indians to be ambitious, avaricious, opportunistic, intelligent, and shrewd businessmen. Malays also have a tendency to look down upon the Chinese as unclean because they eat pork. The same industry and thrift in which the Chinese take pride are regarded as somewhat distasteful, mercenary and materialistic by the Malay.

Stereotypes of the Indian vary. Plantation workers are looked upon as unambitious, lacking in self-reliance and intelligence, while urban Indians are considered shrewd businessmen, though less so than the Chinese. Malays apparently consider Indians rather squalid and are said to find the cooking and body odours of Indians offensive. All three groups tend to look upon fairness of complexion as a sign of beauty.

The handshake is common among men and with close friends one may use both hands to grasp the hand of the other. A more reserved approach is suitable for strangers and recent acquaintances.

In meeting a Malay, the older person should be mentioned before the younger person, the more important before the less important, and the woman before the man. In rural areas, it is not customary for men and women to shake hands with one another. When meeting a man, a Malay woman may *salaam* (i.e., bow low while placing the right palm on the forehead). However, men and women in the cities generally shake hands. The traditional Malay greeting resembles a handshake insofar as both hands are used but without the grasp. The man offers both hands to his friend, lightly touching his friend's outstretched hands and then bringing his hands to his breast. This simply means, "I greet you from my heart."

A white shirt, tie and trousers are acceptable for business calls. A conservative suit should be worn on all government visits. Appointments are necessary for all business firms of any consequence and government visits. Punctuality is expected of Westerners. Shoes are removed before entering a home, and business cards are sometimes exchanged after an introduction.

Acceptance of a dinner invitation is important for the development of good personal relations. Both social and business behaviour are watched carefully and are taken quite seriously by Malaysians.

For beckoning people, the palm of the hand should be turned down and the whole hand waved downward. Never beckon with only one finger. It will be taken immediately as an insult.

Giving and receiving gifts and/or tokens of affection with two hands shows the greatest respect. Objects should not be moved with the feet. A slight bow when leaving, entering or passing by a group is a non-verbal "excuse me" which shows proper respect for the group being passed.

In Malaysia, instead of pointing to a place, object or person with the right forefinger, it is more common to point with the thumb of the right hand with the fingers folded under. In calling for a taxi, one uses the fingers of the right hand, moving them together with the palm facing down in a waving motion. The head is considered to be the centre of the intellectual and sacred power within a person and is not to be touched.

Historical Context

In the fourteenth century, a prince from Majapahit founded the Malacca Sultanate. Malacca became a major trading centre in the lucrative silk and spice trade. In 1511 the Portuguese colonized the area, and a century later the Dutch took control of the colony.

The British established a presence in the area in 1786 with the leasing of the island of Penang by the British East India Company. Singapore was established in 1819. By the end of the 19th century, the British had extended their control to include nearly all of the Malay states as colonies or protectorates.

British Malay was conquered by the Japanese in 1942. After

the war, a revived Malay nationalist movement led to independence from Britain in 1957. The Federation of Malaysia was formed on September 16, 1963 and included the eleven Malay states, Singapore, and the former British colonies of Sabah and Sarawak. Singapore was forced out of the federation in 1965 after tensions grew between its Chinese-dominated government and the Malay-dominated government in Peninsular Malaysia.

During this period, Malaysia was rocked first by Communist terrorism, and then by racial tensions and rioting. Although the government has made great efforts towards rational unity, non-Malay ethnic groups (Chinese and Indians) claim the government is biased against them.

Although Islam is the official religion of Malaysia, Muslims form only 44% of the population. There is a strong relationship between Islam and the state, strengthened by a number of constitutional provisions. Instruction in Islam is provided in all government-assisted schools. Muslims have special obligations as well as special rights under law; they have a separate system of courts and pay special taxes.

Most of the Chinese follow Confucianism, Buddhism and Taoism, while most of the Indians are Hindus. The number of Christians is estimated at about 300,000. The indigenous tribes of Sarawak and Sabah are mostly animist, but substantial numbers have been converted to Christianity.

The economy

The Federation of Malaysia, consisting of the eleven states of the former Federation of Malaya, Sabah and Sarawak, and the federal territory of Kuala Lumpur, was formed in 1963 after the end of the British rule. The population is estimated to be 14 million including 54% Malays, (referred to as *bumiputras*), 35% Chinese, 10% Indians and 1% other peoples, including Eurasians.

The business community has traditionally been dominated by the Chinese, with European firms also playing an important role. The government is currently attempting to redress the economic imbalance between the Chinese and the Malays, but the long-standing racial differences remain.

Education is valued highly and is considered a key to social status and success. Nonetheless, Malaysians usually feel that success and opportunity is due to fate. Family background is often critical to a person's status and the generation of opportunities.

The goal of Malaysian economic policy is to increase the Malay's share of national wealth. Malays control only about 12% of the national wealth. The goal is to increase that to 30% by 1990, with Chinese Malaysians and Indians holding about 40% and foreigners no more than 30%. Therefore, any new foreign investment projects should be joint ventures. Only manufacturing ventures that will produce solely for export can be 100% foreign.

Although economic policy has in practice involved some discrimination, the government does not seek to redistribute wealth by taking away from the Chinese. It hopes to achieve the distribution goals through growth in the economy. Some firms have had difficulty finding enough skilled Malay workers and sufficient Malay capital to finance joint projects. The government also expects foreign firms to train Malaysians to take over management responsibility, reducing the need for expatriates.

The main factors contributing to the growth of the Malaysian economy have been the expanding level of investment (foreign and domestic), increased production of export commodities, and a healthy atmosphere for domestic and foreign private investment.

Only a decade ago, the economy was based almost exclusively on agriculture and mining, but today it is more diverse. Other major sectors of the economy are construction, transportation and communications, wholesale and retail trade, banking, insurance, real estate and business services.

Malaysia is today the world's largest supplier of natural rubber, palm oil and tropical hardwood and related products. Other exports include pepper, cocoa, coffee and vegetables.

The government's active drive for industrialization has resulted in the rapid expansion of the manufacturing sector. Although priority is given to the processing of locally produced raw materials into semi-finished and finished goods, there has been greater success in non-agricultural manufacturing. Activities in this sector range from the assembly of motor vehicles and electronic products to the manufacture of textiles, food, pharmaceuticals and fertilizers, and the construction of off-shore oil exploration and production platforms.

The major trading partners are the European Community, the United States and Japan. As a "middle income" country, Malaysia receives less aid than many other developing countries. The bulk of capital inflow consists of market and project loans from international institutions and the private capital market.

Agriculture is still an important part of the economy, accounting for 22% of GNP, providing 50% of the exports and employing about 44% of the labour force. With a strong agricultural sector supporting it, the manufacturing sector has been able to develop briskly. It now makes up 22% of the GNP while the construction industry, due to urbanization and infrastructure development, accounts for 15% of the GNP.

Mineral wealth has supported the economy and provided for much of Malaysia's strong growth. Natural resources include oil, natural gas, tin, bauxite, iron and copper.

Bibliography

Arberry, A.J., *The Koran Interpreted*. Toronto Canada: The Macmillan Company, 1969.

Evers, Hans-Dieter, *Modernization in South-East Asia*. Kuala Lumpur: Oxford University Press, 1975.

Henderson, John W., *Area Handbook of Malaysia*. Washington D.C.: U.S. Government Printing Office, 1970.

Kasman, Haji Yusof, *"Malaysian Business"*, Berita Publishing Sdn. Bhd.

Kurian, George Thomas, *Encyclopedia of the World: Volume II*. New York: Facts on File, 1978.

Shilling, Nancy A., '*A Practical Guide to Living and Travel in the Arab World*'. Inter-Crescent Publishing and Information Corp., pp. 10-13.

Terpstra, Vern, *The Cultural Environment of International Business*. Dallas: South-Western Publishing Co., 1978.

Renwick, George W., *Malays and Americans: Definite Differences, Unique Opportunities*. Boulder, Colorado: Esso Eastern Inc., 1977.

Language and Intercultural Research Institute, *Culturegrams*. Provo, Utah: Brigham Young University, 1978.

Doing Business in Malaysia. New York: Price Waterhouse and Company, August 1977.

Business Profile Series: Malaysia. The Far Eastern Economic Review, Hong Kong, 1979.

The Far East and Australia 1980-81. Europa Publications Ltd., 1981.

Foreign Economic Trends: Malaysia. Department of Commerce, Washington D.C., March 1981.

Multinational Executive Travel Companion. Boston: Multinational Executive Inc., 1981.

PHILIPPINES

Where personal ties rank high

Filipinos have a strong sense of personal honour, dignity and pride. It is a society where maintaining smooth personal relationships is very important. They have a deep sense of indebtedness, a high sensitivity to insults, and a great reluctance to act in any way that might offend others. A strong sense of social and cultural conformity also exists.

Because of the importance of the family, many businesses are run by Filipino families. Women also enjoy relative success in the business world and near-equal status to men. Indeed, companies are often run by women, whose husbands may merely function as figureheads at board meetings. Filipino women are normally in charge of the money and business operations, a trait seen in their private life as well.

Anthropologists often cite four principal values as the expression of the Philippine value system. They are "*utang na loob*" (a system of reciprocal obligations), "*hiya*" (sense of shame), "*amor propio*" (self-esteem), and "*pakikisama*" (desire to avoid placing others in stressful or unpleasant situations).

Principle of reciprocity: "*Utang na loob*" denotes a sense of personal indebtedness. The understanding of mutual obligation is an important part of Filipino upbringing and it serves as a cohesive force in society. The system is more sensitive or stronger in cases of favours or help (material or non-material) given by one to another. Acceptance of a gift or favour denotes agreement to be obligated to the donor. Repayment of the debt need not be in kind and one must always remember that this is a social obligation, not a "commercial" transaction.

Reciprocity is normally between social equals and serves to

strengthen social relationships. However, it can also exist between superior and subordinate. In this latter case, the subordinate is not expected to reciprocate in equal or greater economic terms (as is usual between social equals), but repayment is enhanced by the subordinate's maintaining the attitude of indebtedness.

Hiya (sense of shame) and the principle of conformity: Hiya serves to enforce correct social behaviour, as shame is associated with violation of social values. Children are, therefore, taught to act in a way that is acceptable within the community. This reinforces the tradition of respect for those in authority and for elders.

Because the Filipino will see a manager as an authority to be respected and obeyed, there will be a tendency to withhold suggestions, questions or comments for fear one might be seen as questioning authority. To accuse a person of not having *hiya* is a grave insult, implying that a person is socially incompetent.

Amor propio (self esteem): Filipinos have a strong sense of pride and place a premium on social acceptance. This makes them extremely sensitive to attacks on their personal honour. For example, an uneducated labourer may not feel his *amor propio* threatened by aspersions on his lack of education, but will be highly sensitive to remarks about his role as husband and father.

Smooth interpersonal relations: Filipino society is highly structured around the principle of smooth interpersonal relations. The ability to get along with others and avoid any outward signs of conflict at almost any cost is cultivated. This attitude is referred to as *pakikisama*. It suggests that the individual should be prepared to go along with a consensus.

Combining this attitude with the traditional respect for authority, it is not hard to see why subordinates will, more often than not, agree with their superiors regardless of their true feelings.

Because of the concern to avoid social friction and minimize potential tensions, go-betweens are often used. Things can be said more readily through and to a third party without being taken as a direct affront.

Benevolent autocracy is a normal style of management, but authority carries with it corresponding obligation. Just as a father wields authority and demands respect from other family members but is equally expected to take care of the family, so are superiors in other aspects of life accorded due respect and also expected to take care of their subordinates.

Filipinos are known for their generosity and hospitality. A Filipino will go out of his own way to please a visitor, and will never accept that he is being inconvenienced by having to do so.

The *suki* system operates to tie business people together with some form of obligation. A trader and a customer will act as each other's *suki*. The trader will offer incentives to his customer such as special prices, credit, preference in case of tight supply of certain goods, and in return the recipient will undertake an unspoken obligation not to trade elsewhere. Though widespread, the practice is restricted to small operations and only where the trader has complete discretion over prices.

A handshake among both men and women is expected upon introduction or greeting of a friend. A common greeting heard in the Philippines is *Kumusta*, which means "Hello, how are you?".

Family discussions

To initiate a conversation, in business or otherwise, it is considered polite to ask first about the family and other casual questions, before getting down to business matters.

When there is considerable difference in years, the older person is shown special respect. In the same vein, when an adult greets a young person, he will do it with the same accord as he would with another adult. A common gesture on the part of the child, in turn, is to take the adult's hand and press it to his forehead.

Business decisions are often made during social occasions such as on the golf course or over a drink and a good meal. Philippine businessmen believe in mixing business with pleasure.

Personal questions regarding the family and other related subjects are usually asked just as a matter of courtesy. They are not viewed as an invasion of privacy, rather as a means of showing concern and interest. Frankness and outspoken expressions are considered rude. All attempts should be made to mask negative or unpleasant feelings.

Filipinos use vigorous hand gestures when speaking, but do

not make physical contact with the other person. Their normal speaking distance is about the same as in the West. They are particularly conscious of maintaining correct posture and proper attire.

To beckon, a Filipino will extend his hand palm down and wave. This gesture is used in calling a taxi and is accompanied by a hissing sound.

Filipinos are vibrant and artistically inclined people who are fond of gaiety, music and social gatherings. Great value is placed on social courtesy. They have an uncanny ability to sense sincerity and are emotional when showing their feelings.

The fact that Filipinos have extended family ties means they tend to socialize much more often with these people and among some intimate friends. If you are invited to a Filipino home, it is customary to bring flowers or a small gift as a sign of appreciation.

A sense of reciprocal obligation is very strong in their culture. If one receives a favour, it must be repaid to the same or a greater degree.

Filipinos are very clean, neat and clothes-conscious. Western fashions have had a substantial impact on their style of dressing.

Normal attire for the man is a shirt called a *barong* for either formal or semiformal affairs. It is a native long-sleeved shirt, semi-transparent for the hot Philippine weather. The man would rarely wear a tie or jacket. Most of the materials are bright and lightweight.

Filipino and English are the official languages and Filipino is the national language. There are also 87 dialects spoken throughout the country, the three major ones being Tagalog (on which Filipino is based) spoken in and around Manila and used by 60% of the population; Cebuano, the language of Viasyas; and Illocano, of northern Luzon. Filipino is taught in the schools and is rapidly gaining popularity, especially around Manila because of its use in the mass media. Because of the former U.S. occupation, Filipinos consider English their second language. It is used by 40% of the population. Spanish is also heard in some parts of the country but only about 2% of the population speaks Spanish, and their numbers are slowly declining.

Indirect or euphemistic speech is often a manifestation of a society's requirement for smooth personal relationships. Verbal manoeuvre is used in stating unpleasant truths or opposing opinions in the most pleasant manner possible. A person will say "maybe" instead of "no". Frank and direct speech is reserved for intimate friends. The Westerner should not, therefore, limit himself to literal meanings of words but analyse also the circumstances under which statements are made.

"Hostess" has a completely different connotation when used in the Philippines. It is used to refer to women who work in bars, cabarets and nightclubs by providing companionship to male customers, an occupation often seen as undignified. Referring to a Filipino wife as a "splendid hostess" therefore is inappropriate.

Historical Context

The Philippines comprise an archipelago of about 7,100 islands of which nine represent 94% of the country's surface. Luzon and neighbouring islands make up the northern sector and Mindanao is the major island in the southern sector.

President Ferdinand E. Marcos remained in power from 1965 until early 1986, when Corazon Aquino was elected President. The President is the head of state and together with the Vice President is elected from the membership of the National Assembly. The President appoints the cabinet and initiates most legislation.

The Philippine population has doubled since it received independence from the United States in 1946, and now totals about 61.5 million. The nation has one of the highest birth rates in the world. Manila, the largest city on the islands, has a population of around 2 million, and Quezon City, the capital, has nearly a million. People have come to the Philippines from many Southeast Asian countries, but the most significant immigrants have the Chinese, who have played an important role in commerce since the 19th century when they first came to the Philippines to trade.

The present culture strongly reflects Hispanic influence, dating from early Spanish domination. The education system, however, was influenced by the presence and the relationship of the Philippines to the United States from 1898 to 1946. Education is highly valued and families will make great sacrifices to educate their children. The literacy rate is approximately 85% and nearly a quarter of the nation's budget is spent on education.

Eighty-five per cent of the Philippine population is Roman Catholic, with Protestants and Muslims representing significant minorities. In addition, there are a number of indigenous religious groups throughout the islands, including the Philippine Independent Church, the Manalistas and Rizalistas. Even though the majority of people profess close adherence to the Christian faith, many cling to folk beliefs in environmental spirits and pagan superstitions.

Religion plays an active role in government affairs and Filipino society as a whole. There are one and a half million Muslim Filipinos, for example, who because of the vast differences in faith and culture, have become quite antagonistic towards the government and the rest of the populace. They live in the southern provinces, which are predominantly poor and unproductive. Insurrections have occurred with regularity. The government has tried on several occasions to offer an amnesty to these people, as well as economic assistance under a general land reform campaign, but to no avail. The Catholic Church has also become deeply involved in governmental affairs by calling for an end to corrupt practices.

The Filipino's pace is slower than the Westerner's. Life is normally relaxed and unhurried. Siestas in the afternoon are common. "Filipino time" usually runs 15 to 30 minutes late, and concessions should be made when setting up an appointment and time for a meeting. In extreme cases, when a visitor is abnormally late, however, every attempt will be made to call ahead with an offer of apologies.

The economy
The United States has traditionally been the Philippines' largest market, purchasing about 36% of the country's exports. Japan is second with about 20% and the European Community absorbs about 15%. Only 11.4% of its total trade is within ASEAN.

The government is also trying to promote trade with socialist and communist countries. In 1976, the first commercial ties were established with the Soviet Union after the beginning of trade with China in 1975.

The trade position has declined sharply since the end of the 1970s. Poor commodity prices have resulted in both lower revenues and lower export volumes produced (also, therefore, increased unemployment). The prospects for Philippine exports continue to be dim. Textiles and electronics are the only major exports not to suffer. The primary government focus on foreign trade is to reduce dependence on imported oil and increase export-oriented industries.

International businesses appear to be returning to the Philippines as President Aquino consolidates her political base. The Philippines' commitment to free enterprise and friendly relations with Western nations remains strong.

The Filipino economy is predominantly agricultural, but manufacturing industries' contribution to the national output has grown in recent years. Five primary products make up more than 50% of the Philippines' visible products: sugar, copper, timber, copra and other coconut products. Imports consist mainly of fuel and manufactured goods, particularly machinery for use in the domestic industries.

Nearly 50% of the 21 million labour force is unemployed or underemployed. Roughly 70% of Filipinos now earn less than the minimum income needed to provide basic food, clothing, shelter, education, transportation and health needs.

High inflation and steep declines in real disposable incomes have been among the major factors depressing private consumption growth in recent years.

Major problems in the essentially centrally planned economy are a rapidly increasing population, heavy reliance on imported oil, high unemployment, and unequal distribution of income.

After the 1972 land reforms, the Philippines gradually became self-sufficient in food production, although import of food has recently increased. Rice is the principal crop, and coconut is the most important export crop. Agriculture employs 50% of the labour force, provides half of Philippine exports, and accounts for 25% of the GDP.

Industry is vital to the economy, accounting for one-third of the GNP and employing 10% of the labour force. The government is encouraging the development of small and medium-size industries, traditionally the fastest growing and the most labour intensive. The boosting of non-traditional export-oriented industries is crucial now that prices for basic exports have fallen dangerously low. The mining industry has suffered tremendously, causing large-scale unemployment in the mining regions. Major new industries have been car and truck assembly, steel, shipbuilding, cement production, timber, textiles and tourism. Manufacturing, however, concentrates on assembly plants and the processing of local raw materials.

Bibliography

A Business Guide to the Association of Southeast Asian Nations. U.S. Department of Commerce, International Trade Administration, March 1980.

Language and Intercultural Research Center, *Culturegrams,* Provo, Utah: Brigham Young University, 1978.

Directory of International Business, Travel and Relocation, First Edition, Detroit Gale Research Co., 1980.

Doing Business in the Philippines. Price Waterhouse Information Guide, March 1978.

F.E.T. — International Market Information Series, "Foreign Economic Trends and Their Implications for the U.S. Philippines," American Embassy in Manila, December 1980.

International Marketing Data and Services, Fifth Edition, London Euromonitor Publications Ltd., 1980.

Language and Intercultural Research Center, *People of the Philippines.* Provo, Utah: Brigham Young University, 1977.

Derek Townsend, *The Philippines.* The Jacaranda Press, 1973.

"The Philippines", *Ernst and Ernst International Series,* Ernst and Ernst, 1978.

Background Notes: Philippines. U.S. Government Printing Office, January 1971.

Vreeland, Nena, et.al., *Area Handbook for the Philippines,* 2nd Edition, American University, Washington D.C., 1976.

SINGAPORE

Instant Asia for Westerners

Singapore has been called Instant Asia because of its great diversity of cultures. The handshake is the most common gesture of greeting, with the addition of a slight bow for Orientals. Hugging and embracing are not typical greetings. In business greetings, it is of utmost importance to address a person with a title such as Mr., Mrs. or Miss. Never attempt to use first names until the other person clearly permits you to do so.

Normally, the host would come out and greet you just outside his office to lead you to the place where you are expected to be seated. After an initial exchange of pleasantries, the host will probably offer you tea, coffee or a cold drink.

Doing business in Singapore is very similar to Europe, and to some extent the United States. Singapore is an industrialized country with a virtual American/European way of life.

Business people from Singapore are known to be rather formal. Superficial smiling is not part of the cultural conditioning of most Singaporeans. They are courteous with people they know, but they don't bother to extend this to strangers. It usually does not mean that they are unhappy or rude, but rather that their courtesy is selective.

The Singapore government is worried, however, that this behaviour could decrease the flow of foreign investors. It has invested heavily in a national courtesy campaign, which has as its theme, "Making Courtesy Our Way of Life".

Foreigners must keep in mind several differences in behaviour. Touching another's head is very impolite. When crossing the legs, one knee is placed directly over the other knee, and the foot or sole should not be pointed at anyone. Foot-tapping or shaking legs under the table while eating or discussing business should be avoided, as this gesture not only denotes feebleness, but also shows loss of interest in the topic or in the person. Moreover, hitting the fist into the cupped hand shows very poor taste. The whole hand is waved, palm down, when beckoning people to come. Never beckon using only one finger. A slight bow when entering, leaving or passing a group of people shows courtesy. During business meetings, self-control and restraint are of utmost importance.

Large companies managed by highly educated Singaporeans usually use Western management systems. However, there remain many small and medium-sized firms that are managed along more traditional lines with a very loose organizational structure and highly centralized decision-making.

Though the English language is widely used in Singapore, the interpretation and understanding of words and phrases differ significantly in some cases from that of the English speakers.

The business communication system is quite similar to that of the West but with many special characteristics, especially in the area of interpersonal relations. If one is planning to visit Singapore and would like to seek business opportunities, it is possible to write an introductory letter expressing interest. Invitations to dinner are frequent. In Singapore business circles, it is very common to show warm hospitality by taking the guest out to the leading restaurants. These evening outings can be seven-nights-a-week affairs. They present an opportunity for both parties to interact on a more social basis.

Smoking is prohibited or discouraged in most public places such as theatres, cinemas. There is a S$500 fine for littering, and jay-walking is also subject to a fine. Traffic in drugs is subject to the death penalty.

The pace of life is fast, and business is conducted expeditiously if the matter requires an immediate decision. Singaporeans are also very punctual and expect others to be the same way. Also, they like to consider the subject of the visit right away, not wasting time with social matters.

When being entertained by a business associate, follow his lead. Avoid topics like local politics and religion. Anti-communist feelings run high in Singapore, and this should be remembered.

When visiting a government official in Singapore, it is customary to attend the meeting wearing a conservative suit. Most other business appointments require a white shirt, tie and trousers. Jackets are necessary in some expensive restaurants at night.

Because of the close historic association with Malaysia and Singapore, Malay is the most widely used language besides English. This is followed by Mandarin and Tamil. All three are considered official languages. English has become one of the official languages as well, and is especially used for business, education and government administration purposes. English is now said to be the predominant language because of its important role as a business language.

Historical Context

Singapore has been self-governing since 1959. The island state formed a part of Malaysia from 1963 to 1965 and became a fully independent and sovereign republic on separation from Malaysia in 1965. In doing so, it became one of the smallest countries in the world.

Singapore is located in Southeast Asia, and Malaysia is its immediate neighbour. It enjoys a warm climate, with a fairly constant average temperature of 26°C all year round. Population is 2·6 million.

Because of its size, Singapore must support the burden of high-density concentration, currently about 3,800 persons per square kilometre. The ethnic composition of Singapore is 76% Chinese, 15% Malay, 7% South Asian. The dominant culture is Chinese although much influenced by its close neighbour, Malaysia.

Singapore is a country of great attraction to international business because of its location in Asia and its free-port advantages. On the other hand, the country faces a labour shortage and sees itself as vulnerable due to its almost total lack of natural resources.

It is a modern trading and industrial country and the major financial centre of Southeast Asia. It has achieved its economic success partially because of its strategic geographic position and its natural harbour. At the beginning of the 20th century, Singapore became a centre for processing imports of rubber and tin from the Malay Peninsula, later developing into a centre of distribution for European manufactured goods throughout the Asian region. When Singapore became independent, its previous economic structure was changed in order to enlarge the domestic market. The main features of its economy still relied on international trade and the flow of goods from the Western region to Asia. The major factors that contributed to the remarkable economic growth of the country were the competitiveness of its export products, its ability to attract overseas investment, and finally the development of a highly sophisticated financial sector.

Singapore has now achieved a standard of living approaching that of Europe. Its port ranks fourth in the world, and its petroleum-refining capacity is third. Entrepôt trade is still an important part of the economy, but it is clear that the future trend is directed more towards the manufacturing sector and the maintenance of its financial centre.

Singapore, with only 238·5 square miles, rates as one of Southeast Asia's smallest yet most unusual countries. A young nation, with approximately 40% of its people under 19 years of age, Singapore has conducted rigorous family planning programmes to stabilize population growth, and overpopulation is no longer seen as a future problem.

Of Singapore's three main ethnic groups, the Malays tend to be the least successful economically. In fact, the Chinese and Indians average almost twice as much in monthly income. The Chinese have retained their entrepreneurial traditions, and many are self-employed businessmen. They also, as do the Indians, tend to hold a high proportion of the government, technical and professional positions.

Singaporeans live in relative racial and religious harmony. The country enjoys a thriving and growing middle class. Its multi-ethnic background has been successfully woven together through the government's multiracial policies, which have mandated integration in the armed forces, public schools and public housing. Singapore has subsequently emerged as a city-state with an identity which has withstood the social and racial pressures inherent in this society.

The family is still an important social unit. The average Singaporean household numbers about six members, with three generations commonly living together. As in many countries, those with lower incomes usually have the larger families. The professional in Singapore generally has but two children. Family loyalty and trust are important values in this society. Respect for the elderly, especially one's own, flavours the life of this Asian city-state.

The middle class is burgeoning in Singapore. The great disparities in wealth that were once common are now disappearing. More and more people of every ethnic heritage are reaping the benefits of Singapore's prosperity.

Singapore enjoys freedom of worship. The four main religions are Islam, Buddhism, Christianity and Hinduism, and all are practised widely. Buddhists are the most numerous.

In order to reduce religious problems, an inter-religious organization was established to promote the spirit of friendship, cooperation and goodwill among all religions.

The government is exceptionally stable. The PAP, People's Action Party, which tends towards a social democratic stance, was formed in 1954, and has remained in majority control since 1959, when Singapore became an independent republic under self-rule.

Foreign policy is centred on ASEAN, of which Singapore is a charter member. The position of Vietnam and the Kampuchea questions are the major issues. Relations with China are close. Singapore's political ties are neutral.

The economy

Singapore's major trading partners are Malaysia, Japan and the United States, in that order. The main commodity imported by Singapore is petroleum, which accounts for more than one-fourth of the total imports. Other important imports include electrical components and appliances, which make up more than a tenth of all imports.

From the export point of view, the commodities are the same: approximately one-fourth of the total export is petroleum, and one-tenth is in electrical machinery and appliances. The difference between these imports and exports is the finished product. Petroleum arrives in its raw form, and leaves Singapore refined. Electrical machinery and appliances are imported in pieces and are assembled in Singapore, in order to be finally exported as finished goods. Overall, the trade position is good and external debt is moderate.

Although the current account has continuously been in deficit, long-term capital inflows help keep the overall balance of payments account in surplus. Capital inflows will cover the deficits with no problem.

Main exports include tin, rubber, copra, petroleum (refined), coffee, coconut oil, palm oil, pineapples, iron and steel, leather goods, textiles, telecommunications equipment, transportation equipment, machinery, electrical components, television and radios, clothing and chemicals.

Main imports include machinery and transportation equipment, manufactured goods, raw materials, chemicals, edible oils, rice, sugar, fuels, petroleum and electrical components.

About 120,000 foreign workers, mostly Malaysian, are employed in the economy. The government's goal is to completely eliminate guest workers by the 1990s, either by not re-employing them when contracts expire or by offering citizenship to essential workers.

Singapore's powerful economy is supported by a strong international financial and communications centre. In addition, the government has encouraged the growth of non-traditional export-oriented industries. The public sector is active and strong, and accounts for about 22% of the GDP. But the government exerts relatively little control over the economy. The Economic Development Board provides incentives for export-oriented industries, aids in project proposals and studies, and provides some manpower training. The government's primary goal is to provide an attractive environment for high technology industries. In fact, in recent years traditional industries such as textiles have been surpassed by higher technological industries like oil rig construction, transportation equipment, precision instruments and chemicals.

Singapore is not well endowed with natural resources, but has made the best of its good location. Infrastructure is well developed as well as the communication and financial networks.

The manufacturing industries are well-developed, diversified and growing rapidly, accounting for about one-fifth of GNP and employing 30% of the labour force. 60% of all manufactured goods are exported. Because of government building programmes and infrastructure development, the construction industry is booming. Five per cent of the labour force is employed in construction.

Services are vital to the economy. The number of hotels and tourist accommodation and services have all been expanded. As an international financial centre, Singapore is mighty, although competition from Hong Kong is intense. Financial services account for almost half of the GNP.

Agriculture plays only a minor role in the economy, and its importance is declining. Land under cultivation is sparse, and less than 5% of the labour force is employed in agriculture.

Stable investment environment

The Singapore government's stability has increased the number of interested foreign investors and, in turn, the government has enhanced this appeal by providing a warm welcome for foreign investors, successful development of physical and institutional infrastructure, and a hard-working labour force. A positive economic environment and an array of generous incentives designed to attract investments have combined to produce growth and diversification.

The Singapore government's main policy is to raise the standard of living and ease the tight labour market. The policy includes three years of wage increases, and emphasis on skills development, a new incentive for research, capital investment, computerization and training.

The government is a principal economic force both as employer and as initiator and manager of development projects. Its efforts to forge national unity based on a distinct set of Singaporean values and attitudes is of equal importance in the role of the government. It actively promotes multiracial harmony, hard work, austerity, sacrifice and continuing vigilance against external threats.

Over the next few years there will be a striking shift away

from the government's traditional role as a prime mover behind Singapore's progress.

Three immediate implications for companies:

1. The government will gradually sell off its minority shares in firms and publicly list many companies in which it owns a majority interest.
2. Companies will face less competition from state-owned businesses in coming years and find the government an increasingly reluctant joint-venture partner.
3. The government will allow market forces free rein in determining which industries should survive.

Bibliography

Nena, Glen, Geoffrey, Peter and Shinn, *Area Handbook for Singapore:* First Edition, 1977.

Area Handbook for Singapore. United States Printing Office, Library of Congress, 1977.

Doing Business in Singapore. Price Waterhouse, 1978

Economical Foreign Trends for Singapore. United States Government Printing Office, 1981.

Hodgkin, Mary C., *The Innovators.* Sydney University Press, 1972.

Marketing in Singapore. Overseas Business Reports, July, 1977.

Republic of Singapore. Culturgram Communication Aid.

Background Notes on Singapore. September 1978.

Singapore: Facts and Pictures, 1980. Information Division/Ministry of Culture, Singapore.

Business International: Asia Pacific Forecasting Services. Singapore, May 1986

Heidt, Erhard U., *Television in Singapore: An Analysis of a Week's Viewing.* Inst. Southeast Asian Stud., Gower Pub. Co., 1984.

Brailey, Nigel, *Thailand & the Fall of Singapore: The Frustrating of an Asian Revolution.* (Special Studies Ser.), Westview, 1985.

Clammer, John, *Singapore: Ideology, Society, Culture.* Advent, NY: Chopmen Singapore, 1986.

Wee, Jessie, *We Live in Malaysia & Singapore.* Bookwright Press, 1985.

SOUTH KOREA

Asia's 'vertical' society

An important concept to understand for working in Korea is *kibun*, one of the dominant factors influencing conduct and relationships with others. The word literally means inner feelings. If one's *kibun* is good, one functions smoothly and with ease. If one's *kibun* is upset or bad, then things may come to a complete halt. The word has no true English equivalent, but "mood" is close. In interpersonal relationships, keeping the *kibun* in good order often takes precedence over all other considerations.

In business functions, businessmen try to operate in a manner that will enhance the *kibun* of both persons. To damage the *kibun* may effectively cut off relationships and create an enemy. Indeed, one does not do business with a person who has damaged one's *kibun*.

Proper interpersonal relationships are important and there is little room for equality in relationships among Koreans. Relationships tend to be almost entirely vertical rather than horizontal, and each person is in a relatively higher or lower position. It is essential for one to know the levels of society and to know one's place in the scheme of things. In relationships, it is often necessary to appear to lower oneself in selfless humility and give honour to other people. A well-respected Korean often assumes an attitude of self-negation and self-effacement in social and business contacts. To put oneself forward is considered proud arrogance and worthy of scorn.

Protocol is extremely important to Koreans. When meeting others, if you do not appreciate a person's actual position and give it due recognition, he might withdraw on some pretext and try to avoid future contact.

A representative of another person or group at a meeting is treated with even more care than that person or group because the substitute may be sensitive to slights, real or imagined, and report it back to his colleagues. This is very difficult for Westerners to understand, but a Korean who fails to observe the basic rules of social exchange is considered by other Koreans to be less than a person — he is a "nonperson".

All foreigners, to a certain extent, are considered by Koreans as nonpersons. Koreans show less concern for a nonperson's feelings or his comfort; he is not worthy of much consideration. When relationships are broken among Koreans, some people tend to resort to violence, but every effort must be made to remain within the framework of polite relationships.

Elders in Korean society are always honoured and respected. To engender the anger of an elder means serious damage, because his age allows him to influence the opinions of others, regardless of the rights or wrongs of the situation. In the presence of an elder, one remains at attention, not even smoking or drinking. Like children, elders must be given special delicacies at meals, and their every wish and desire is catered to whenever possible. The custom of sending the elderly to "rest homes" is considered barbarous and shocking by the Koreans. Every home in Korea, no matter how poor, allocates the best room in the house to the honoured grandfather or grandmother.

Essential etiquette
In personal relationships with strangers or associates, Koreans tend to be very strict in observing the rules of etiquette. To touch another person physically is considered an affront to his person, unless there is a well established bond of close friendship or childhood ties.

In modern South Korean society many businessmen now shake hands, but they will often bow at the same time. To slap someone on the back or to put one's arms around a casual acquaintance or to be too familiar with someone in public is a serious breach that may effectively cool future relations.

It is not the custom among Koreans to introduce one person to another. Instead, one would say to another, "I have never seen you before," or, "I am seeing you for the first time." The other person repeats the same thing, and then usually the elder of the two persons in age or rank says, "Let us introduce ourselves." Each person then steps back a little, bows from the waist, states his own name. They are then formally introduced. Names are stated in a low, humble voice that may not be heard accurately, and calling cards are exchanged. One may learn the new person's name and position at leisure. Do not say, "Sorry, I didn't catch your name. Would you tell me again?" Calling cards are necessary in South Korea, and should be utilized by businesspeople at all times.

The use of names in Korea has an entirely different connotation than in most Western countries. To the Confucian, using a name is presumptuous and impolite, as a name is something to be honoured and respected. It should not be used casually. In Shamanism, to write a name calls up the spirit world and is considered bad luck. A name, whether it is written or spoken, has its own mystique, and is regarded as personal property. To call someone directly by his name is an affront in most social circumstances.

In Korea, there are relatively few surnames, thus there appears to most Westerners to be an inordinate number of Kims and Parks. A Korean is addressed by his title, position, trade, profession, or some other honorific title such as teacher. As opposed to saying, "Good morning, Mr. Kim," a polite "Good morning" is better. Many Koreans work and live next to each other for years without even knowing their full names. The president of South Korea is referred to by high officials as "Excellency", even in his absence, because it is considered too familiar to use such a high person's name in conversation. A Korean's name is usually made up of three characters — the family's surname is placed first, and then the given name, which is made up of two characters. It is used by all members of the same generation.

To embarrass someone by making a joke at his expense is highly resented, even if done by a foreigner who does not understand the customs.

After a few drinks, businessmen often become very affectionate, but at the same time apologize for being a bit drunk.

The next day they will tell their colleagues that they are sorry for imposing on their good nature while being a little tipsy.

Several other points to keep in mind are:

1. It is necessary to schedule business and government appointments in advance.
2. Business cards should be printed in English and Korean.
3. Although Koreans lavish entertainment upon their guests, the visiting businessman should be aware that his behaviour is being discreetly tested at social functions.
4. Before entering a colleague's home, or a Korean restaurant, the visitor should remove his shoes.
5. The Koreans are justifiably proud of their rich history and culture.
6. Topics to avoid include local politics.

In business, flattery is a way of life. Without subtle flattery, business would come to a halt. One must begin on the periphery in business relationships and gradually zero in on the main business in narrowing circles. To begin directly with a discussion of some delicate business matter or new business venture is considered by Koreans to be the height of stupidity, and dooms the project to almost certain failure. Koreans view impatience as a major fault. A highly skilled businessman moves with deliberation, dignity and studied motions, and senses the impressions and nuances being sent to him by the other businessman.

To Korean businessmen, Western business people often appear to make contracts on the assumption that all the factors will indefinitely remain the same. They take a gamble that society will allow them to complete the agreed conditions of the contract. In Korea, a written contract is sometimes of little value, though this is currently changing. It may be only a paper contract, and there may be no understanding that it will be kept if the conditions at the time it was made should change. A change in the economy, the political situation, or the personal will of one of the contractors may invalidate the completion of the contract without any sense of misdeed.

Table manners are based on making the guest feel comfortable. The attitude of a servant is proper for a host with his guest. At meals, the hostess is at the lowest place, the farthest from the place of honour, and often will not even eat in the presence of a guest. Before beginning to eat, the host will often make a formal welcome speech stating the purpose of the gathering and paying his respects to his guest.

Often food is served on small individual tables, each with many side dishes of food, a bowl of soup, and a bowl of rice. One removes the top of the dish of the hot rice and places it on the floor under his place at the table. Korean food tends to be highly seasoned with red pepper, thus a careful initial taste of the soup is advisable.

To lay the chopsticks or spoon on the table is to indicate that you have finished eating. To put them on the top of a dish or bowl means that you are merely resting.

A guest may show his appreciation for the meal by slurping his soup or smacking his lips. Guests are not expected to clean their plates, and to leave nothing indicates that you are still hungry and embarrasses the host by implying that he has not prepared enough food. The host will continue to urge his guest to eat more, but a firm refusal is respected. A good healthy belch after a meal is a sign that one has eaten well and enjoyed it.

Giving and receiving

Koreans give gifts on many occasions, particularly where business interests are involved, and the appropriate etiquette surrounding the giving of gifts is often a problem for Western businesspeople. In this context, every gift expects something in return, and one rarely gives an expensive gift without a purpose. The purpose may be to establish an obligation, to gain a certain advantage, or merely to create an atmosphere in which the recipient will be more amenable to the request of the donor. To return a gift is considered an affront, but in some instances it may be better to return the gift than to accept it with no intention of doing a favour in return.

Some Koreans have a special ability to work their way into the affection of foreigners and form personal relationships that may later prove embarrassing and/or difficult to handle when some impossible or illegal request is made.

In Korean, "yes" may merely mean "I heard you," and not agreement or intention of complying. To say "no" could hurt the other's feelings, and thus is poor etiquette. Koreans often say "yes" to each other and to foreigners and then go on their own way doing quite the opposite, with little sense of breaking a promise or agreement.

A gift of fruit or flowers is appropriate whenever one visits someone's home, but other gifts are not opened in front of the giver. In both offering and receiving gifts it is customary to use both hands.

The establishment and maintenance of social ties is of extreme importance to Korean businessmen. It is believed that a good social rapport must be established between two parties before any serious business is transacted.

Avoiding overt anger

Harmony in personal relations and conversation dominates Korean attitudes. The dignity and self-esteem of a colleague is of paramount importance to the Korean. Consequently, an outward show of anger or emotion is to be avoided.

When conversing, proper posture is emphasized. Hands-in-pockets relaxed posture is not acceptable. In Korea, men do not touch one another during a conversation unless they are very close friends.

South Korea is a mountainous country, and the climate varies with altitude. The winters are cold and the summers hot. Temperatures range from below freezing to above 90°F. Snow will fall in the capital during winter but will usually not stay on the ground for long. Autumn and spring are the most enjoyable seasons. Temperatures are moderate both day and night.

When travelling to Korea during the winter, it is advisable to pack a medium-weight topcoat. Light-weight clothing is appropriate for the summer season. Business attire for both men and women is formal. A conservative suit is suggested.

The Korean language, called Hangul, is a simple, concise and efficient means of writing. It is a phonetic alphabet system consisting of 24 letters and can be learned in a few hours of intensive study. The spoken language, however, is a very complex embodiment of the cultural and class distinctions that have existed for more than 2,000 years. For example, verb forms will differ depending on the formality of the occasion or the person being addressed. This complexity and sensitivity to the culture makes mastery of the language by foreigners very difficult.

Language lesson

Basic Expressions:

Anyong hashimnika? (Literally "Are you at peace?") This is the basic greeting comparable to "Hello, how are you?"

Pangapsumnida. "I'm happy to meet you." This is used to return a greeting when first meeting someone.

Anyong he chou mou sha sumnika? "Good morning! Did you sleep well?"

Chal maw gaw sumnida. (After a meal) "I ate well."

Kam sa hamnida. "Thank you."

Mi an hamnida. "Excuse me. I'm sorry."

In general, the quality of sanitation in Korea is not good. Water purification systems are not always adequate. Water should be boiled, especially in rural areas. Sewage and garbage systems are confined to cities.

Precautions should be taken when purchasing any fresh meats, vegetables or fruit. All fish must be cooked very thoroughly before it is eaten.

The main dishes at a Korean meal are boiled rice and *kimchi*, a hot, spicy dish of which there is an endless variety made with cabbage, turnips, cucumbers, scallions, etc. *Pul Kogi* is a barbecued-beef dish that is frequently cooked at the table. *Sinsollo* is a regal casserole of vegetable, eggs and meat also cooked at table. A festive table will also contain a variety of cooked and raw vegetables and roots as well as fish dishes.

The traditional drink in the countryside is called *makoli* and is a thick, white rice brew frequently made at home. The more refined rice wine (*chong jong*) and beer are also popular. The host traditionally pours the first drink for his guest, who is expected to drain the cup and return it to the host and pour him a drink.

While knives, forks and spoons are always available, a visitor who has mastered the use of chopsticks will delight his host. A variety of fruit is usually served as dessert.

Throughout Seoul, there are good supermarkets that carry locally produced items. Bargaining for prices is generally accepted, but stores are beginning to establish set prices.

The government operates a number of commissaries for foreigners that stock a variety of consumer goods from overseas such as cigarettes, liquor, canned goods and toiletries.

There are some good, but expensive, Western restaurants in the better hotels. A 15% luxury tax and 10% service charge are usually added to the bill, so tipping is not necessary. Korean business associates usually entertain men only. This is done in Korean restaurants or *kisaeng houses* (the Korean equivalent of a Japanese Geisha house).

Historical Context

Korea, formally known as *Tai Han Min Kuk* (The Country of the Great Han People) is popularly called "The Land of the Morning Calm". Since 1945, the nation has been divided into a northern zone called the People's Democratic Republic of Korea and a southern zone called the Republic of Korea (South Korea).

South Korea covers 38,211 square miles, or about 45% of the Korean peninsula. Its low, rugged mountains are devoid of forest cover. The winters are long, cold and dry. The summers are short, hot and humid, drenched by a rainy season in July and August.

The population is estimated at over 42 million. Seoul, the bustling capital city, is located in the northwest corner. Pusan, on the southeast coast, is a special city headed by a mayor who is directly responsible to the central government. Urban population exceeds rural population by 65% to 35% respectively.

The legend of Tangun relates that in the 24th century B.C., the son of the Creator turned a bear into a woman and mated with her, producing an offspring named Tangun who descended on Kangwha, a large island off the coast of Inchon, and became the ancestor of all the Korean people.

Modern archaeological findings indicate that the earliest Korean peoples were migrants and invaders from present-day Manchuria, Northern China and Mongolia some time before the 11th century B.C.

Throughout much of the 2,200 years of their recorded history, the Korean people have found themselves trapped between powers greater than themselves. From the late 4th century to the mid-7th century A.D. the peninsula was divided into three kingdoms: Koguryo in the north, Paekche in the southwest, and Silla in the southeast. Unified in the Silla Kingdom (676—935 A.D.), Korea was dominated by its stronger neighbour, China. This domination continued during the Koryo period (935—1392 A.D.) and included the takeovers by the Mongols.

Again, during the Yi dynasty (392—1910) the Korean peninsula became the battlefield for wars between China and Japan, and later in the conflict between Tsarist Russia and Japan.

Japanese colonial rule over Korea from 1910 to 1945 is often remembered with bitterness by Koreans. A pragmatic decision by the United States and the Soviet Union in 1945 divided Korea at the 38th parallel when they accepted the surrender of Japanese forces. Although national reunification is a goal of both zones, it is not foreseen in the near future.

Since the end of the Korean War in 1953, South Korea has experienced the uncertainties and stresses of extraordinary economic and social change. The underlying ethic of Korea is Shamanism, but the people have also been strongly influenced by Buddhism and Confucianism. Shamanism is the religion of ancient Koreans for whom the elements of earth — mountains, rivers, etc — were sacred. Shamanism was introduced to Korea in the 4th century and has the longest history among the organized religions in Korea. Confucianism has also been a strong force, and the most influential of the newer native Korean religions is Ch-ondo-gyo, which was founded in the mid-19th century on the belief that every person represents heaven. Christianity was introduced into Korea in 1783 by Korean diplomatic delegates who came into contact with the Bible in China. About 28% of the population is now Christian.

South Korea is one of Asia's most densely populated nations. This predominantly Buddhist country has a 90% literacy rate, and 40% of South Koreans live in cities of over 100,000. Seoul has a population of 9·6 million, while Pusan (3·5 million), Taegu (2·0 million) and Inchon (1·4 million) house much of the rest of the country's urban dwellers.

The South Korean people are an unusually homogeneous

race. Most are of Mongol or Tungusic descent, with some Chinese mixture. They are to be distinguished from other Asians by their broad foreheads and height.

South Korea is a socially stratified society. The establishment of proper social and business relationships is of extreme importance to Koreans, and Confucian teachings have had a great impact on Korean attitudes and values. Rituals of courtesy are ever-present, and formality in behaviour is the rule. Public modesty, when speaking of one's family or achievements, is the norm, and harmony with one's family, friends, and business colleagues is important.

In Korea the family unit is emphasized, with the elders occupying a special and honoured place. Duty and obligation bind members of the family together. Several generations may live in the same household, although this is less and less true for Westernized city dwellers. Women have a distinctly unimportant role in this patriarchal system.

The State Council is the highest policy-making organ of the nation. It is composed of the President, the Prime Minister and no more than 30, no fewer than 15, other members. The Prime Minister is appointed by the President and must be approved by the National Assembly.

The government's policy goals are stabilizing the domestic political situation, strengthening the national security capability, improving social welfare, and achieving balanced societal development.

The executive branch of the government is composed of two boards and 18 ministries. Planning and development is accomplished through a series of Five Year Plans.

The economy

The government wants to reduce the gap between the rich and the poor. There will be a changeover from direct government control in the economy to an economy run by market forces. The economy will continue to be led in growth by exports, but the aim is to export more technological and sophisticated goods. Incentives to develop technology include a 10% corporate tax break.

Major projects include the expansion of one international

airport and the building of another. The shipbuilding industry will also be heavily promoted.

The assassination of President Park in 1979 and the recession in 1980 plus political unrest have hurt South Korea, but some stability has returned.

South Korean strengths are good entrepreneurial skills, an educated and disciplined labour force, and good infrastructure. Only technology is lacking. The goal is to make exports more sophisticated in content and to move away from cheap consumer goods, which are facing increased protectionism in the West. Electronics is currently the fastest-growing industry.

The new government development plan aims for growth with stability and the greater welfare of the general population. The current focus is on promoting heavy industry, which provides a large portion of total Korean exports. The government wants the economy to move from a high growth economy to a more moderate and stable one. The focus will be on making structural changes needed in the transition from the boom years of the 1970s.

The country's energy policy is crucial to South Korea's economic progress. Coal will be the key element and production efficiency will be improved as South Korea tries to reduce its dependence on oil. Nuclear power and natural gas sources will be developed.

South Korea successfully exports clothing and textiles, electrical equipment, ships, iron and steel, footwear, fish, machinery, metal products, electronics and synthetic resin products. Imports include petroleum, fuel, wood, foods, wheat, rice, cotton, textile machinery and chemicals.

A recent growth in exports has resulted in new jobs for over 2 million people. Employees in the export industry account for over 50% of the total workforce.

The unit of currency in Korea is the *won* and exists in 1, 5, 10, 50, and 100 *won* coins and 500, 5,000 and 10,000 *won* notes.

Full-service foreign banks operate in Korea and *won* can be exchanged for foreign currency only when departing from Korea. Circulation of foreign currency is illegal.

South Korea's top 10 export destinations are the United States, Japan, Hong Kong, Canada, West Germany, Saudi

Arabia, Britain, Panama, Singapore and Norway. These 10 accounted for approximately 75% of Korea's total exports.

In recent years, the national economy has fallen below the government's original target. The growth rate has been attributed to the shaky external trade climate, which has resulted primarily from the trend towards protectionism and the overall stagnation in the advanced countries, which are Korea's major trading partners.

Internally, Korea has failed to reach its projected growth rate due to low consumption and inactive investments in fixed production facilities.

The flow of outside funds

A great number of foreign investment projects have been authorized in recent years. Principal investors are by rank: Japan, United States, Hong Kong, Britain, West Germany and Saudi Arabia. Major areas of investment have been in the hotel and tourism industry and in manufacturing and mining.

South Korean construction companies have developed internationally recognized techniques. Under the Five-Year Development Plan, they have undertaken huge projects, including construction of dams, highways, tunnels, and factories. Construction orders have increased both domestically and abroad.

An emerging trade surplus will continue in the near future and enable Seoul to boost its foreign exchange reserves while working off some of the large accumulated debt of past years.

After 1984, the Labour Ministry designated labour-management cooperation and employment stabilization as two of the basic tasks for government. Other tasks included improving labour conditions and workers' welfare, strengthening vocational training and preventing workshop accidents.

To sell in Korea, it is useful to have the assistance of a Korean registered agent. All registered agents (there are over 2,000 such firms) belong to the Korean Traders Association (KTA). The "Exalted 13" are Korea's 13 General Trading Companies (GTC) and are powerful within the Korean economy.

Bibliography

Allen, Horace Newton, *Things Korean*. New York: F.H. Revell Publishers, 1973.

Hamilton, Angus, *Korea: Cultural Interpretations*. New York:
C. Scribner's Sons Publishing, 1974.

Wickman, Michael, *Living in Korea*. Seoul, Korea: American Chamber of Commerce in Korea, 1978.

Crane, Paul S, *Korean Patterns*. Seoul, Korea: Royal Asiatic Society, Korea Branch, 1978.

Kim, Young "Yun, Inter-Ethnic and Intra-Ethnic Communication: A study of Korean Immigrants in Chicago." *International and Intercultural Communication Annual,* 1977, IV, 53-68.

Anderson, Carolyn and Carven, Maureen, *Living in Korea*. Honolulu; Albert M. Newman Enterprises, 1974.

Vreeland, Nena et al. *Area Handbook for South Korea*. Washington, D.C: U.S. Government Printing Office, 1975.

Koreans: Building Bridges of Understanding. Provo, Utah: Language Research Center, Brigham Young University, 1976.

Karl Chun editor, *Korean Annual 1986*, 23rd ed., copyright 1986, Yonhap News Agency.

Business International: Asia Pacific Forecasting Services, Korea, May 1986.

Yu, C.S. & Guisso, R., *Shamanism: The Spirit World of Korea*. (Studies in Korean religions & Culture), Asian Human Press.

Covell, Jon C., *Korea's Colorful Heritage*. Si-sa-yong-o-sa. 1986.

Michell, Tony, *Simple Etiquette in Korea*. Norbury Pubns. Ltd., 1985.

Yoon, Hong-Key, *Geomantic Relationship Between Culture and Nature in Korea*, 2 vols. (Asian Folklore and Social Life Monographs: vol. 88), Oriental Bk. Store.

Steinberg, David I., *South Korea Profile*. (Profiles-Nations of Contemporary Asia Ser.), Westview, 1986.

Morse, Ronald A., editor, *Wild Asters: Explorations in Korean Thought*, Culture & Society. Woodrow Wilson Intl. Center, U. Press of America, 1987.

TAIWAN

A strategy for growth

One absolute necessity for doing business in Taiwan is the business card. Ideally the front of the card should carry your name, company name and address in Chinese characters. The back of the card should have the English equivalent. Cards are exchanged not only in business settings, but also on social occasions. A plentiful supply may be necessary. The cards can be ordered and printed in a day or two at any of the printing shops in Taiwan. If one plans an extended trip to Taiwan, a seal, or "chop" is also helpful although not essential. The seal will contain the Chinese characters representing your name. Using the chop serves the same purpose as affixing a signature for the Chinese.

The selection of a proper Chinese name is essential. The meaning of the individual characters and their combined meanings are considered to bring luck and symbolize a person's inner character. In traditional China, parents went to great lengths to cast horoscopes and consult with local scholars in order to select an auspicious name for their children. When first introduced, Chinese people will often discuss their names, commenting on the meaning of the characters individually and of the name as a whole.

Most Chinese names are three syllables, or three characters long. The first syllable character is the surname, while the last two characters represent the given name. Thus Li Tzu-shan's family name is Li and his given name is Tzu-shan. Foreigners from the West may refer to him as Mr. Li.

Modesty is one of the most valued characteristics in traditional Chinese culture. Direct criticism, boisterous behaviour and bragging about past achievements are to be avoided.

"Face" in Taiwan, as in any Chinese society, is of prime importance, and Westerners are often perceived as having little grasp of the social and cultural behaviour needed to protect an individual's honour and privacy. Anger or any sign of displeasure with performance is best expressed indirectly. Unrestrained display of emotion is a sign of immaturity and vulgarity.

Authority in Taiwan is based on status and age. Consensus decision-making is not a part of the system. The directives of superiors are usually respected, to the extent that they are seldom questioned. With growing democracy in Taiwan, this may be changing.

Many businesses in Taiwan are family controlled and the patriarch is the unquestioned decision maker. In the case of major decisions, other family members and relatives will be consulted.

When first meeting someone, a slight bow of one's head and a handshake are considered appropriate. Elderly persons are always recognized and greeted first. If invited to someone's residence, it is appropriate to bring a small gift, such as fruit. Both hands should be used when handing a gift or other object to another person. Shoes are usually removed before entering a home, and slippers are worn inside unless the host tells you to do otherwise. When leaving, the guest bows to his host. The host will usually accompany the guest a fair distance from the home; to this the guest should give only a token resistance.

In Taiwan as in China, one does not point with the index finger, but rather with the open hand. It is common for friends of the same sex to hold hands, despite age. Eye contact should be established.

In a business situation, expect to spend a fair amount of time discussing matters not related to your actual business concerns. For example, the Chinese invariably serve hot tea to guests (no matter what the weather) and the guest may find himself at an initial encounter discussing no more than the merits of Chinese tea as compared to Bombay tea. Other favourite topics of conversation include Chinese history and food. These discussions are not meant to detract from the business purpose of the meeting, but rather to set a proper and friendly atmosphere in which negotiations may be carried out.

At all costs, avoid offering direct criticism in conversations and negotiations. The Taiwanese are generally quiet and reserved, and any abrupt or untactful behaviour is unconstructive.

If invited by a Chinese host to dinner, the host will expect to pay the bill. The guest, on this first occasion, may make an attempt to pay, but in the end graciously allow the host to win out. If invited on subsequent dinners, the host will again attempt to pay, but at this point it is best that the guest seriously attempt to pay. This is best done by arranging in advance that you are hosting the meal.

The Chinese host may also offer to pay for taxi cabs, trains, and other incidental costs. The guest should attempt to pay for them. Keep in mind that an initial attempt to pay will be refused, and that a second or third attempt is necessary.

Eating and drinking

It is considered a friendly act to share drinks with friends or business acquaintances. Several things should be kept in mind, however. The Chinese generally do not dilute liquor or make "mixed" drinks. Whatever liquor is ordered will be served straight. The traditional Chinese toast is *gan bei* (bottoms up). The proposer of the toast will drain his glass, but guests are not obliged to follow the example. Drinking beyond your limit is acceptable and is a sign that you are at ease.

An appreciation of fine cuisine is important to the Chinese. They serve good food to close friends and respected customers. Always compliment the food, especially the great number of dishes (even if there are only a few) and inquire as to the origins and preparation. The Chinese will use chopsticks to eat, although most restaurants will provide knives and forks upon request.

By Western standards, dress in Taiwan is conservative, especially for women. In practically all business dealings, men will wear Western style suits and women should take special care to dress appropriately. For men, a light-weight conservative business suit with a white shirt is recommended.

Ideas of fashion and style may not always be in keeping with European or U.S. tastes. The older generation of Taiwanese businesspeople will sometimes mix and match colour combinations and styles that, to the Western eye, may be considered a poor selection.

In the north, the summer is warm and humid from May to October. January and February are cold and rainy. In the south, the weather is warmer, but it can turn chilly between December and February. Typhoons are a problem from June to October, and they can be severe.

The best time for business travel is from September to May. Avoid the two weeks before and after the Chinese New Year, the Dragon Boat Festival (May-June) and the Mid-Autumn Festival in September or October. Every four years, the lunar calendar has 13 months instead of 12.

Historical Context

Portuguese sailors in the 16th century named the island of Taiwan Ilha Formosa, meaning Beautiful Island.

Over time, the island has been occupied by Spanish, French, Dutch and Japanese colonists. The Dutch colonists were ousted by the Chinese in 1661, and in 1684 Taiwan was made a prefecture of China's Fukien Province.

The island was ceded to Japan following the Sino-Japanese War of 1895, and remained under Japanese control until the end of World War II.

In 1949, the successes of Mao Zedong's Communist forces forced Generalissimo Chiang Kai-shek's nationalist government to retreat to the island of Taiwan. Mao's plans to invade Taiwan in the 1950s were thwarted by the Taiwanese army, which was assisted by the U.S. 7th Fleet.

Although the government in Taiwan has claimed to represent all of China, the People's Republic of China was admitted to the United Nations in Taiwan's place in 1971. Official diplomatic relations with the United States were severed in 1979 as a result of normalized relations between Washington and Beijing. Relations do, however, continue between the U.S. and Taiwan on an informal basis through the American Institute in Taiwan.

Taiwan is an island just 240 miles long and 85 miles wide at its maximum point. It is 100 miles east of the mainland of China and about 700 miles south of Japan.

Population is about 20 million, with the capital, Taipei, accounting for over 2.2 million. The people are predominantly Chinese, most of whom are descendants of immigrants from southeast China or mainlanders who retreated to Taiwan in 1949. The original inhabitants number only about 150,000.

Mandarin is the official language, but the Taiwanese dialect is also widely used.

Moral standards are high and the Confucian ethic, including filial piety, still dominates the national ethical code. Public displays of affection are rare.

Education is free and compulsory until about the age of 16, and literacy is nearly universal.

The principal religions in Taiwan today are Taoism and Buddhism. Buddhism is numerically superior with some 3,000 Buddhist temples for some five million devotees. Protestant Christians number about 320,000 and they maintain about 1,000 churches. There are roughly 300,000 Roman Catholics with 600 churches. The Muslim community is relatively small, with some 40,000 adherents and 12 mosques.

The economy

Foreign trade is vital to Taiwan's economy. The government is targeting electronics, chemicals, biotechnology and machinery for development as exports. Growth in these areas will also cause imports to increase as technology and capital will have to be imported. Taiwan is also aiming to diversify her export markets.

Taiwan's trade account typically runs a comfortable surplus with the United States particularly, while trade deficits are run with Japan. To even these accounts out, Taiwan has recently encouraged a "buy American" campaign.

Exports continue to drive the economy. Export contribution to GDP peaked at 64% in 1984 but is predicted to fall to 53% by 1990.

The monetary unit is the New Taiwan Dollar (NT$) divided into 100 cents. The New Taiwan Dollar circulates in coins of one and five dollars and notes in denominations of 10, 50, 100, 500, and 1,000 dollars. The metric system is used, but some markets still use the old system of measurement.

Despite setbacks in its international status, Taiwan has

continued to prosper and to enjoy political stability and economic growth. Only about 20 countries maintain diplomatic relations with Taiwan, but trade relations are being established with more countries each year.

The 1970s saw agriculture, long the leading element in the national economy, surpassed by industry. Industrialization was begun by the Japanese and its growth accelerated in the post war era. Government-owned enterprises include aluminium, cement, coal, fertilizer, machinery, paper and sugar.

The private sector is loosely regulated by a government advisory committee responsible for overseeing production, but its main purpose is to promote foreign sales. The leading privately owned industry is textile manufacturing. In order to promote economic development, the government aids private enterprise to employ new techniques and locate foreign investment.

After more than 30 years of tight control, the government is beginning to relax. President Chiang Chien Kuok, who died in February 1988, had been replacing older bureaucrats with younger politicians, most of whom have been educated in the United States. Politically Taiwan remains fairly isolated. Most nations have moved their embassies to Beijing. Taiwan has been forced out of the IMF and the World Bank. However, Taiwan now attends ADB Board meetings again and economically the country is far from isolated. Although Taiwan's officials still refuse to address the mainland government officially, informal links continue to grow.

Energy insufficiency remains one of Taiwan's most serious problems. Eighty-five percent of the country's energy needs are imported. The new development plan slates energy conservation as a prime target. Coal and nuclear power use are both targeted to increase. Taiwan is preparing to build a fourth nuclear power plant on the island.

The government has sought to develop strategic industries, encourage and, in some cases, force more research and development. More training for skilled workers and specialists is being provided, and the government is continuing to invest heavily in technology related to defence.

Taiwan has removed virtually all exchange controls, and import tariffs have been greatly reduced.

The country will continue to welcome foreign investors, even in new areas such as local consumer markets and the services sector. Joint venture terms are becoming increasingly negotiable. Indeed many U.S., Japanese and Hong Kong firms have already entered the market. More liberal trade, investment and financial rules will help increase foreign investment in Taiwan.

The government's new policies towards business will be to enhance the competitiveness of exports, promote the transfer of advanced technology, and above all, try to boost private investment. The last aim will be tackled partly through easing up the monetary policy, forcing down interest rates and making more credit available (by encouraging banks to liberalize terms). The government is willing to trade mild inflation for a partially invigorated economy.

Specific policies will be to encourage capital-intensive high-technology firms, rather than labour-intensive industries. There will also be less government protection for domestic firms and more direct government assistance to targeted industries. The government also plans to reform public firms, reduce bureaucracy and strive for more efficient management.

Bibliography

Li, K.T., *The Experience of Dynamic Economic Growth on Taiwan.* Taipei, Taiwan: Mei Ya Publications, Inc., 1976.

Moore, C.A., *The Chinese Mind.* Honolulu: East-West Center Press, 1967.

U.S. State Department, *Background Notes: Republic of China.* Washington, D.C.: U.S. Government Printing Office.

Yu, K.H., "New Challenges to our Economy." *Economic Review,* January — February, 1981.

Investment, Licensing, and Trading Conditions Abroad Taiwan. Business International: New York, March, 1986.

Lanier, Alison, *Update-Taiwan.* (Country Orientation Ser.), Intercult Pr., 1982.

Living in Taiwan: 1985 Edition. Augsburg, 1986.

Gold, Thomas B., *State & Society in the Taiwan Miracle.* M.E. Sharpe, 1986.

Li Wu, Yuan, *Becoming an Industrialized Nation: ROC Development of Taiwan.* Praeger, 1985.

Gates, Hill, *Chinese Working-Class Lives: Getting by in Taiwan.* (The Anthropology of Contemporary Issues), Cornell U. Press, 1987.

Harrell, Stevan, *Ploughshare Village: Culture & Context in Taiwan.* (Publications of the School of International Studies on Asia: No. 35), U. of Washington Press, 1982.

THAILAND

Enjoying life

The Thais believe life should be enjoyed. Problems and setbacks should not be taken too seriously. This endows the Thai worker with a kind of happy-go-lucky attitude that can be both fascinating and frustrating to outsiders.

Doing business in Thailand can result in major problems with the Thai people if local business customs and protocol are not taken into account. Probably most disturbing will be the Thai's smiling assurance that you will get exactly what you want when you want it, followed by delays or even complete inaction. Situations of this nature can best be understood by remembering the Thai emphasis on harmony as well as the country's *mai en rai* ("never mind") attitude. When you combine the two, this response makes sense.

The Thai culture is a very unusual mixture of the two dominant cultures of the Asian region: Indian and Chinese. Indian influences can be seen in the Theravada Buddhism, which reflects the Hindu concern for the future and little of the Chinese secular concerns.

Religion plays a very important part in the life of the Thai people. There is evidence of this in the large number of monks attending to religious and social affairs in and around Bangkok. Theravada Buddhism, which is the principal religion, has strong ties to the people and the state. The *sangha* (Buddhist clergy) have often been called on by the state to convey important messages to the people and have at times welcomed the state's protection. In times of moral crisis, the *sangha* serve as the moral backbone of society.

The centre of religious worship, especially in the provinces, is the Buddhist temple, or *wat*. In rural areas both religious and educational instruction may be provided at the local *wat*.

Certain customs and courtesies must be observed in Thailand. For example, the head, as the highest part of the body, must be treated with respect. Never pat anyone on the head or place your hand over the back of another's chair. Never pass objects over the heads of people who are seated. As for the feet, they are the lowest part of the body and it is considered impolite to point your foot at someone. Other actions to be avoided are stamping the feet, touching other people with your foot or placing your feet on the desk when your are in a meeting.

Foreigners must learn to bargain. Rarely are the prices correct as marked (except possibly on food) and haggling for souvenirs, taxi rides and other daily expenses is considered standard business procedure. One should decide approximately what price to pay for an item before one attempts to acquire it.

Cajoling and any other forms of persuasion short of shouting are permissible. One should always be ready to leave if the negotiations are not going well. Often the threat of the loss of a sale is enough to induce a sudden change of heart in the merchant. After all, the taxi driver knows another taxi will be right behind him. It is in these bargaining sessions that a little knowledge of the language can be most helpful.

Payoffs, kickbacks and commissions have been part of the Thai business system for years. Though there have been recent efforts to crack down on such corruption, it is still an accepted way of doing business. Foreign companies often employ a local businessman whose knowledge of government protocol can keep activities running smoothly. Two reasons are often given for the large-scale corruption within the business and government communities. One is the inadequate salaries of the government officials; the other is the Thai love of the good life, or *sanuke*.

The traditional form of Thai greeting is called the *wai*. Though the handshake is used in business dealings and between members of the higher social class, most Thais use the *wai* to greet one another. The *wai* is performed by holding the hands in a praying position with fingers extended and placing them on the chest. The higher the position of the hands on the body, the greater the respect indicated for the person being greeted. Thus, placing one's hands on the forehead shows extreme respect. Usually the *wai* is accompanied by a bowing motion — a slight bending at the waist. A *wai* should be returned immediately, otherwise it is a sign of disrespect.

When being introduced, Thais generally use both their first and last names in that order. It is common to address associates by their first name preceded by Khun which means, Mr./Mrs./Miss. Take extra time in learning the names of important business contacts, preferably before the meeting. It will be gratefully appreciated.

Thai is the most common language. It is a tonal language, meaning that the same sound with different intonations can mean vastly different things. For example, the word *mai* can mean anything from "wood" to "no". English is also spoken, as are Chinese, Malay and Vietnamese by the respective minorities.

It is customary to wear a dark conservative business suit when keeping an appointment with a government official. For business meetings, a shirt, tie and trousers are usually acceptable.

Western-style dress is common in Bangkok. However, the typical clothes for the Thai women are a blouse and a long ankle-length skirt called *pa-toong*.

Because of their outgoing nature, it is very easy to make friends with the Thai people; but when conversing, it is best to use caution when talking about leaders, religion or the country. It is particularly important that the King and the Royal Family only be referred to with the greatest respect. The Thais love sports, especially kick boxing, horse-racing, soccer, and *tah-Kraw* (a volleyball-like game played without using the hands). The Thais enjoy people with a sense of humour, but reserved behaviour in public is a must.

Most of the population is ethnically Thai, with Chinese (7%) and Malay (3%) forming the only substantial minority groups.

Historical Context

Thailand has a land area about the same size as the U.S. state of Texas and a population of approximately 54 million. The terrain is mountainous along the western border and in the northwestern quadrant, descending into fertile plains in the eastern Mekong and Chao Phraya river valleys.

The weather has been described as "heat interspersed with periods of rain" — in other words, Thailand has a tropical monsoon climate. March, April and May are the driest and hottest months, when the average temperature is in the 90°s Fahrenheit (32° centigrade). The cool season, with temperatures in the mid-to-low 80°s Fahrenheit (27° centigrade), lasts from November to February.

Thailand means "the land of the free". The Thais are proud of the fact that they have never been under Western domination, though all the surrounding nations have at one time or another been colonies. This can be attributed to both the resourcefulness of the Thai politicians and the willingness of the Thai people to accommodate outsiders within the political structure.

The government has extensive connections with the military. A number of politicians are also military officers, and government coups are often brought about because of internal struggles with the military for power.

The political situation was, in the past, typified by short-term governments and bloodless military coups, which are actually less upsetting in Thailand than are elections in other countries. The military wields considerable power, and no government is able to survive without its support.

Difficulties in Viet Nam and Laos are still threatening, and border skirmishes are not uncommon. For this reason, considerable military influence is likely to be maintained for quite some time. The inflow of refugees has been a severe economic drain on Thailand's resources.

Thailand is a constitutional monarchy. However, the King has increasingly become a key figure on the political scene, as he is the only person able to break the impasse between opposing interest groups. Practical politics are handled by the most powerful politician, the Prime Minister, who serves a four-year term. The National Assembly is divided into a Senate and a House of Representatives. Traditionally, the National Assembly has played a secondary role in government, many times serving as a rubber stamp for the Prime Minister and his council of ministers.

About 85% of the people speak a dialect of Thai. The

overwhelming majority are poor rural dwellers. Metropolitan Bangkok (population about 5.5 million) is by far the country's largest city. The next largest urban centre is the provincial town of Songkhla, with 173,000 inhabitants.

Thailand's economic and social structure is controlled by three different groups: the bureaucracy, the military, and the business community. Of these three groups, the Chinese are present only in the business community.

There is a small middle class, consisting of the well-to-do bureaucrats and the successful shopkeepers. Otherwise, there is a great disparity in the ways Thais live. The rural poor have maintained a low standard of living literally for centuries.

The economy

State enterprises consist of a number of wholly or partly owned industrial monopolies, such as electricity generation, water supply, the Thailand Port Authority, the telephone service and rail transportation. Each enterprise provides substantial business opportunity for foreign interests. The country is a member of ASEAN, the Association of South East Asian Nations.

The business community sees the Thai market as divided into three principal areas: the state-owned enterprises, the national government market and the local governmental market. All these divisions overlap, with no real clear-cut division. The manufacturing sector accounts for most of the remaining jobs. Most of the production is earmarked for domestic consumption, especially in the areas of cheap consumer durables.

Mining has been a small sector of the Thai economy. Tin, precious stones and minerals such as tungsten, lead, antimony, manganese, copper and zinc have been the principal mining products. Increased oil and natural gas production, as well as hydroelectric production, have slightly eased Thailand's energy dependence.

But agriculture is the real backbone of the economy. It provides 60% of export earnings, employs 70% of the labour force, and accounts for 25% of gross domestic product.

Some 25% of Thailand's population lives below the world poverty line. Political power is centred in Bangkok, and has succeeded in keeping much of the national wealth there.

Consequently, rural income averages only about 30% of the median income in Bangkok. In the long run, major structural changes will be necessary to ensure continued self-sufficiency in food production. Land reforms are needed to provide incentives for the small farmer to produce more.

Although Thailand is rich in minerals, with deposits of limestone, lignite coal, gemstones, copper, iron ore, zinc and salt, only tin is mined extensively.

Thailand is heavily dependent on imported oil, which supplies 80% of energy needs, with the remainder provided by coal and hydroelectric power. The development of natural gas reserves should help in further industrial development. The gas is expected to last at least 50 years.

The development of industry began with import-substitution, and is now nearly fully achieved. The government is concentrating now on promoting export-oriented and labour-intensive industries. Thailand's labour costs are still relatively low, even in comparison with the rest of the developing nations in Asia, so the country has attracted outside industry.

Bibliography

Bickner, Robert J., et al., editors, *Papers from a Conference on Thai Studies in Honor of William J. Gedney.* (Michigan Papers on South & Southeast Asia: No. 25) Ctr S&SE Asian, 1986.

Keyes, Charles F. Thailand: *Buddhist Kingdom As Modern Nation State.* (Profiles-Nations of Contemporary Asia Ser.) Westview, 1987.

Moore, Frank J., et al., *Thailand: Its People, Its Society, Its Culture.* (Survey of World Cultures Ser.: No 15), Bks. Demand UMI.

Fraser, Thomas M., Jr., *Fishermen of South Thailand: The Malay Villagers.* Waveland Press, 1984.

Lewis, Paul & Lewis, Elaine, *People of the Golden Triangle: Six Tribes in Thailand.* Thames Hudson, 1984.

Prasithrathsint, Suchart. *Ethnicity & Fertility in Thailand.* Institute of Southeast Asian Studies, Gower Pub. Co., 1986.